Also from Westphalia Press
westphaliapress.org

The Idea of the Digital University

Dialogue in the Roman-Greco World

The Politics of Impeachment

International or Local Ownership?: Security Sector Development in Post-Independent Kosovo

Policy Perspectives from Promising New Scholars in Complexity

The Role of Theory in Policy Analysis

ABC of Criminology

Non-Profit Organizations and Disaster

The Idea of Neoliberalism: The Emperor Has Threadbare Contemporary Clothes

Donald J. Trump's Presidency: International Perspectives

Ukraine vs. Russia: Revolution, Democracy and War: Selected Articles and Blogs, 2010-2016

Iran: Who Is Really In Charge?

Stamped: An Anti-Travel Novel

A Strategy for Implementing the Reconciliation Process

Issues in Maritime Cyber Security

A Different Dimension: Reflections on the History of Transpersonal Thought

Contracting, Logistics, Reverse Logistics: The Project, Program and Portfolio Approach

Unworkable Conservatism: Small Government, Freemarkets, and Impracticality

Springfield: The Novel

Lariats and Lassos

Ongoing Issues in Georgian Policy and Public Administration

Growing Inequality: Bridging Complex Systems, Population Health and Health Disparities

Designing, Adapting, Strategizing in Online Education

Secrets & Lies in the United Kingdom: Analysis of Political Corruption

Pacific Hurtgen: The American Army in Northern Luzon, 1945

Natural Gas as an Instrument of Russian State Power

New Frontiers in Criminology

Feeding the Global South

Beijing Express: How to Understand New China

Demand the Impossible: Essays in History as Activism

Lights and Shadows of Quakerism

by Edward Ryder

WESTPHALIA PRESS
An Imprint of Policy Studies Organization

Westphalia Press
An imprint of Policy Studies Organization
1527 New Hampshire Ave. NW
Washington, D.C. 20036
info@ipsonet.org

ISBN-13: 978-1-63391-848-1
ISBN-10: 1-63391-848-3

Cover design by Jeffrey Barnes:
jbarnesbook.design

Daniel Gutierrez-Sandoval, Executive Director
PSO and Westphalia Press

Updated material and comments on this edition
can be found at the Westphalia Press website:
www.westphaliapress.org

LIGHTS AND SHADOWS

—OF—

QUAKERISM

—BY—

EDWARD RYDER

PAWLING, N. Y.
PHILIP H. SMITH, PRINTER
1886

PREFACE.

Neither the Christian Public nor the World at
large has ever adequately understood the phenome-
non of Quakerism. It was a powerful movement in
the direction of freedom of conscience and spirituality
in religion—one of those numerous bursts of theistic
force which in different ages have set the currents of
human thought flowing on higher levels. The movement was marred near its commencement by certain
peculiarities, and finally checked by a too rigid in-
crustation of the red-hot lava of reform, producing a
new repression of the freedom the movement came to
assert. This was due partly to the unripeness of the
age, and partly to the nature of the minds acted
upon. A century later Methodism met with better
success by taking a less advanced position and holding it with more practical regard to the wants of the
masses. The Quakers allowed their zeal to master
their discretion, and by insisting on a too absolute
standard of propriety shut themselves off from the
multitude and stood still till the world went by them.
Nor were they aware when the changes took place
which left them contending about non - essentials

while the less punctilious divisions of the great army
of the Cross moved on to the important business of
saving souls. At length they began to perceive that
what they had supposed to be their special and distinguishing doctrine, the light and guidance of the
Spirit, was becoming the common creed of the
Church. Active work and the steady rising of the
Millennial Day had brought the general intelligence
forward to a recognition of truths once apprehended
by only a few persons.

Probably this common race-advancement goes on
under certain general laws and influences, with much
less dependence on local displays than we are apt to
suppose. Bright days are a result of Spring, and not
Spring a result of bright days. These early sun-
bursts often come weeks before the steady June
weather. Then follows the certain reaction, and then
another leap forward. We should not order it so,
but that is God's fashion of putting away the wintry
weather.

The following brief essays are designed to indicate
both the advance and reaction in the great spiritual
movement which occurred in the latter half of the
seventeenth century. So rapid was its progress that
in a few years England, Scotland, Ireland and the
American Colonies were strongly tinged with the
new doctrines, and several societies had been planted
on the European Continent. The battle for liberty
of conscience was fought and won, this time without

"carnal weapons." The name given in derision, became a title of respect. Wealth, ease, social position
followed, and then came the reaction to a conservatism more stringent than that recently overpowered,
followed by a decline as phenomenal as the sudden
rise of the Society. The causes of this Decline have
been the theme of numberless discussions both within
the Body and among interested onlookers. A certain
mystery seems to envelop the subject in most people's minds, giving it a kind of fascination apart from
its serious importance. Naturally those most concerned cannot rest while doubtful of the causes that
are paralyzing their best efforts to preserve their
beloved Society and keep their children from stray-
ing into other folds.

This is another attempt to answer the inquiry in a
way that may be beneficial not only to Friends but
to others who can see a providential purpose in setting forth a beacon light for the advancing divisions
of the Church Militant—a standard of spirituality
perhaps in advance of what will be generally practicable for some time to come, but which, with its attend-
ant dangers of excess, may profitably be kept in view
by those who aim at intelligent and safe progress in
religious culture.

Quaker Hill, N. Y., May 1, 1886.

CONTENTS.

LIGHTS AND SHADOWS OF QUAKERISM.

I.

THE INNER LIGHT.

When George Fox turned in holy disgust from the blind teachers to whom he had vainly applied for help, to the Light of Christ in his own soul—"the true Light which lighteth every man coming into the world"—and thus found "One who could speak to his condition," a new sunrise dawned on the era of the Protestant Reformation. There had been other prophets and other bright arisings in this new spring-time of reform, but none that promised better fruits from a humble beginning than that which brought Christ Jesus again to be the recognized Teacher of his waiting disciples.

Hitherto the Bible, as interpreted by the Church, or by human reason, had been regarded as "the only and sufficient rule of faith and practice." Now the living WORD OF GOD, who was before all worlds, came to be looked upon, not only as the needful Illuminator of the written *words of God*, but as capable of opening the mental eye of the faithful believer through the immediate touches of that heavenly Beam which originally gave light to the prophets and apostles.

This was esteemed by theologians of the time a
dangerous and fanatical assumption, and in rash
hands it might have proved such; but young Fox
and his friends seem to have had wisdom given
them to guard against the peril by bringing their
alleged revelations, or "openings," to the test of
the written Word;—not as to a superior rule, but
to a corroborating witness: and they freely acknowledged that whenever a supposed revelation plainly
conflicts with the "Scriptures of Truth" it must
be rejected. Without such a limitation all would
have been at sea again; for with no acknowledged
standard of judgment, one man's "revelation" has
the same authority as another's. But thus guarded
the doctrine is rendered safe, and differs from the
common theory only in its account of how the conscience and understanding become enlightened. According to the Quaker doctrine conscience is the
moral eye of the soul; but it is at first blind,
through sin, and at all times powerless without
the living light of Christ to endow it for action.
Neither the Bible nor any human teacher can do
this without the Sun of Righteousness; while He
can do it even without these instruments, however
useful they may be as helps and reflectors of His
true, or living, light. They believe that He who spoke
to Adam in the garden, and to Saul on his way to
Damascus, is still able to address the heart and
conscience of man, without being limited to any

particular medium. At the same time they recognize the value of the Scriptures whenever they
are available; and that in most instances, though
by no means always, the voice of the living Teacher
comes in connection with words stored in the
memory, or traced on the page of Holy Writ,—so
vitalizing these as to give them present authority.
This is the common method of learning the will
of God among Bible readers; but how, where the
Bible is not read? Is God altogether silent, or
without a witness, to the ignorant masses of men?
By no means, say the Friends. "The heavens de-
clare the glory of God, and the firmament showeth
His handiwork: there is no speech nor language
where their voice is not heard." Not only this,
but "The grace of God which bringeth salvation
hath appeared unto all men, teaching the denying
of ungodliness." Hence, as the air and the sunlight give life to men's bodies, so the secret breath
and light of Christ everywhere quickened their immortal spirits. Dimly indeed shines the heavenly
beam where it has not made for itself a tabernacle
in human speech; but still, with "fair and friendly
ray," it warms and keeps alive the moral nature,
adding so much of the substance of life eternal
as the heart will receive—enough to bring many an
Arctic flower to bloom, and gather, throughout the
ages, a vast multitude, babes and little children
though they be, "from the east and from the

west, from the north and from the south," to "sit
down with Abraham, Isaac and Jacob in the kingdom of God;" while many who, on account of
their external knowledge, think themselves pillars
in that kingdom, will be cast out.

Such is the doctrine of the *Inner Light*, or as otherwise expressed, the "Universal and Saving Light of
Christ." The endowment it gives is not a part of
man's proper, or hereditary nature, but is rather the
germ of a higher nature which enters his being
through faith and elevates it to the spiritual rank.
When not thus born of Christ man remains in spiritual darkness, even though some degree of moral virtue invests him with those preparatory graces which
invite the higher life of God.

It is interesting to notice that a truth thus clearly
enunciated more than two hundred years ago by the
Friends is now being slowly recognized by our "advanced thinkers."

Meantime its early advocates permitted a shadow
to gather over their path by failing to hold the truth
in moderation. So enamored did they become of
their favorite doctrine that they suffered the great
earthly repository, or verbal incarnation of the light
of past ages, and other useful learning to fall somewhat below par in their estimation. This was after
the founders of the society had rested from their
labors. They used the Bible freely and with great
power, often taking it as a sword in their hand, in

their public ministry. The sword which is wielded
by the Spirit of God has a double edge, the Living
Word being one side and the Written Word the other; and to do effective work both edges should be
used. It was therefore a serious loss when the Scriptures ceased to be read in the public assemblies; for
then the spirit had far less power "for reproof, for
correction, and for instruction in righteousness," than
had they been wisely used under its direction. It
was no doubt the fear that they would be read formally, and thus interfere with the silent part of worship, or the direct promptings of the Spirit, which
caused their removal. But that certainly was not an
adequate reason for so great a change. The clear eye
of George Fox foresaw the danger, and to warn his
brethren he is said to have nailed a Bible in the house
where he worshipped. But the reproof and warning were without avail. His followers remembered
his famous watchword, "*Mind the Light*," and tried
in their way to keep their lamps burning; but with
the golden candlestick removed, and but an irregular
supply of oil for their lamps, it was not long before
the silences grew formal and wearisome to the common people, the sermons became hackneyed and repe-
titious, prayer was often but the silent pressure of
the soul upward, and the song of praise was heard no
more. So the unconvinced who had no mental store
to draw upon went away, to return only when a speaker
of note was announced.

To-day hundreds of Friends' Meeting houses are falling into ruins in this land of liberty because the Light which ceases not to "enlighten every man," when not excluded or suppressed, has failed to find competent light-bearers within them. A portion of the Society have learned the important lesson that God works with means, and adapts those means to the condition of the people, using the candlestick with the candle, and applying both edges of the sword; and those are going on with renewed pace—albeit sometimes they break into an unquakerly trot. But even a torchlight procession, with drums beating in the name of the Lord, after the style of the Salvation Army, or a brisk Methodist gallop toward New Jerusalem is a much more pleasing sight than empty benches, closed doors and churches falling to decay. Such methods would indeed be unseemly for plain Friends, and might repel those whom milder means would win; but is there not a medium course which would be approved of true wisdom, because happily combining in fruitful and more constant radiance the responsive beams of the Outer and the Inner Light?

II.

THE HEAVENLY GUIDE.

If God thus communicates with His children is it not reasonable to suppose that through this inshining Light of the Spirit, not less than by revelations previously made, He will govern His church and guide His willing servants? So trusting, Friends besought their Heavenly Leader to direct all their steps—especially in their religious engagements. Not blindly, by a hidden Providence, would they have this done, but intelligibly, as a father speaks to his children. "No longer do I call you servants;" said Jesus to his disciples; "for the servant knoweth not what his lord doeth; but I have called you Friends: for all things that I have heard from my Father I have made known unto you." This is the high privilege of all who walk in the Spirit, that they are taught of the Lord, according to the words of the prophet, "I will put my law into their minds and write it in their hearts; and I will be their God and they shall be my people."

A belief so honoring to Christ's gospel was not without its fruits. One after another the illusions by which Satan held in thrall, not only worldly-minded

people, but many half-enlightened Christians, were
laid bare, and step by step the meek band of those
who loved their Lord's appearing were led from the
wilderness of traditional opinions and customs into
the open walks of truth and righteousness.

The reforms thus inaugurated were often of the
most radical character. No respect was paid to
existing customs, however strongly established, merely because such were the usages of the Church, or of
society. The paths of Primitive Christianity were
again sought out, and Spiritual Religion, pure, simple and rational, was offered to the people in the
name of the crucified, risen, and returned Saviour.

Nor can it be denied that their testimony was accompanied "with demonstration of the Spirit and of
power." Multitudes were converted to the new
faith. Not only did the messengers tremble like
wires charged with electricity, but often a whole
assembly would be shaken; and at times their per-
secuting accusers and judges were also constrained
to "tremble before the Lord." So common were
these tremulous motions, as when Sinai quaked
beneath the lightning and thunder of God's presence, that the name Quakers became their common
appellation. The title bears honorable witness to
their sincerity, and the respect of Him who, when
His disciples formerly were united as one soul
and voice in earnest prayer, shook the place where
they were gathered together, "and they were all

filled with the Holy Ghost." Alas that the experience should have become so rare among Christians as to make it a distinguishing title, and even a fancied stigma. But patience had its reward, and the title at length became a badge of respect.

As we have seen, the doctrine of the immediate revelation of God's will to His people proved revolutionizing. It does not belong to the doctrine, if admitted, that results will always be the same. Here is where the Quakers, in time, carried the reform to excess by insisting so strongly on uniformity of opinion and practice among those governed by the Spirit that finally they become oppressors in turn. All we we can say, while acknowledging that "there are diversities of gifts, but the same Spirit, and differences of administration, but the same Lord, and diversities of operations, but the same God who worketh all things in all," is that herein God wrought effectively to produce a certain type of Christian experience and faith. And probably it will now be admitted by most intelligent Christians that the world has been benefited and the cause of true religion advanced not a little, through the developments thus made. Our present task is to trace these developments and also to note the apparent excesses and reactions attending them, for the benefit of those interested.

The Quakers, or Friends, as they prefer to be called, felt obligated to wait, often a long time for the "openings," "impressions," or "motions" of the

Spirit, before engaging in any religious service.
Certain general duties were excepted, such as meeting
together at stated times; though extremists demand a special prompting for even this duty.   When
gathered, instead of proceeding, as most Christians
do, to read, pray, sing, and preach, they waited
for a special impulse to each and all these acts, feeling
that "the preparation of the heart in man and the
answer of the lips are from the Lord;" that acceptable worship cannot be offered in man's will;
and that Christ being present, should direct the
exercises of the meeting, assigning to each member
his appropriate duty.   All therefore sat in silence
until some mind felt impressed to give utterance to
its thoughts, emotions, or desires.   Experience
proved that sometimes one, sometimes several, and
occasionally none, would feel thus impressed.   A
great variety of experiences was thus presented,
according to the constituents of the meeting; but
duty done was the chief reward of all, and that
done silently was believed to be equally pleasing to
God.   Mistakes were of course frequent, but these
the good Father knew how to pardon, while gently
leading His little ones along the ascending road
to His house of many apartments.

Whatever we may conclude in regard to the particular way in which Friends were led, the beautiful doctrine of God's paternal guidance must ever commend itself to the heart of the Christian.   The only

occasion for wonder is that the directions we receive
should be so indistinct as they are to most of us.
This may be due to various causes; chiefly no doubt
to the imperfect state of our spiritual faculties. The
prophetic gift is rare, and yet we all have rudimenta-
ry organs of perception by which we can in time, perhaps, distinguish the guiding pillar of cloud, or fire,
as it moves silently on before us. Let us hope the
day is not distant when, through the combined power of growth and education our spiritual sight and
hearing will become so acute that we can not only see
the Son of Man as he comes in the clouds of heaven,
with all his holy angels, to judge the living and the
dead, but can also "hear a voice behind us," as we enter the streets of New Jerusalem, saying, "This is
the way, walk ye in it."

There is, however, another possible cause for the
indefiniteness of the directions we now receive. The
child that is shown how to solve every problem in
his arithmetic seldom makes a good mathematician.
God does not wish us always to be children in understanding. "In malice be ye children, but in understanding be men." How should we become men
if told distinctly just how to perform every act—
when, where, and how to do every simple duty? At
first we must be told plainly, each time. Then as
memory and reason begin to develop, rules take
the place of specific commands. Finally the principles underlying those commands and laws are dis-

cover'd, and we are asked to apply these principles
to the determination of a proper line of conduct, and
at length to the particular steps of that line. When
difficult questions arise we have our teachers, and
even the President of the University, to apply to for
relief; but our wise Father does not wish our path
made so plain, except at the beginnings of our course,
that we shall not need to think. It is often best
for us to think hard and long, to wrestle with
the problems before us, to come almost to de-
spair. Thus reason, judgment, faith, hope, perseverance, are all made strong. Thus, and thus alone,
can we become men.

If we examine God's method of training the human
race we shall perceive that in matters of religion as
well as common conduct such has been His plan of
education. First He appeared to Adam and the pa-
triarchs and told them precisely what to do, and what
not to do. A basis thus laid down, He then wrote out
a series of rules, embodying the instructions previously given into a system. Finally He transformed
the written code into a spiritual law in the form of
recognized principles of conduct. This constitutes
the Gospel dispensation.

During each administration special helps were afforded at the beginning: just as in entering on a new
study the teacher gives special attention to his pupil,
and illustrates each principle for him. These personal attentions and illustrations form the miracu-

lons periods in which God stooped down to earth and
wrote with His finger on the ground of man's physical
senses, thus awakening new perceptions and ideas.
When mental forms or images have been thus created they soon reproduce themselves in language
and begin a new circle of activities, always of a
more advanced kind. We thus have a dispensation
of personal government, in the patriarchal age; a
dispensation of law, from Moses onward; and a dispensation of principles, introduced by Christ and carried forward by the Spirit.

Now in applying this to the individual life the
same order will be discovered. First, we are shown
distinctly what we shall do, and what leave un-
done. Then rules of behavior are given us. And
finally, as men, we are expected to see what is proper
and do it, without particular instruction.

A fair inference for the case we are considering
would seem to be that the special directions we at
first receive from our spiritual Guide are to be gradually wrought into a body of principles to be used by
the enlightened understanding as occasions arise,
the Spirit working more and more with our spirit,
through our improved faculties, and by more orderly methods.

I think there is no doubt that such are the teach-
ings of experience with most people; and it is quite
possible that a habit of depending on special promptings for the performance of general and easily per-

ceived duties, and teaching the uninitiated to look for some mysterious token of the Divine will before putting the hand to the plow, or setting bread on the Lord's table, may have had much to do with the dearth and barrenness so often lamented among Friends. We are not justified in working without God; and yet we *must work*. If the thing that should be done is not done, the fault is ours: and since it only makes matters worse to work blindly, we must get help to open our eyes, and set us rightly forward. If the Lord seems to be asleep in our vessel, we must waken him; for that is not faith which sits still and does nothing. It was his disciples' fear that he chided—not their faith in him; for he answered their call and stilled the tempest. He can also break the calm if we will pray to Him and *spread our sails*.

III.

The soul of worship is love. Without genuine love to Go·l in the heart all forms of worship are a shadow, or a pretense. And yet Christianity has often been so often misconceived that an empty ceremonial was supposed to be acceptable to God, and a discharge of the highest duty known to man. One who reads the history of the Middle Ages, and of England to the present century, can but be astonished at the blank ignorance of the masses, high and low, who in the midst of their godless debaucheries and brute struggles for mastery turned at stated times to the "sanctuary" of Him whose "eyes are too pure to behold iniquity," and, apparently without the least doubt of their acceptance, "performed Divine worship" with great solemnity and punctiliousness. Indeed, up to the time of the rise of Friends, the opinion seems to have been general that worship consisted largely, if not mainly, of external acts. Of course there were those who knew better, just as there were thousands, all through the dark ages, who saw and loathed the abominations of Popery; but the prevailing conception was grossly sensuous and formal.

Against these abuses the Quakers drew forth the two edged sword of the Spirit and made clean work of them all, proclaiming again the words of Jesus, "*God is a Spirit, and they that worship Him must worship Him in spirit and in truth.*" What priestly ritual, or fixed order of proceedings could stand under this rule? If the heart must not only accompany, but must inspire every utterance before it can reach the heart of God, how can people with unwashed hands come into the Lord's presence and begin using the sacred vessels which have been consecrated to a pure service—the solemn words of prayer and praise, and holy exhortation which befit only lips touched with living coals from God's holy altar? If Moses was required to put off his shoes before the burning bush, and the sons of Aaron must be themselves clean, and offer no unclean beast unto Jehovah, how much more should they who come into that Temple which is sanctified, not with "the blood of bulls and goats," but of God's own unspotted Lamb, bring only a pure offering.

What attitude so becoming in those who thus approach the Mercy-seat, as that of reverent silence, with head and heart bowed in humble waiting until God shall cause His glory to appear between the cherubim of adoring Faith and Love, inspiring hope, joy and thanksgiving? Then let the song of praise ascend, as pure incense from the golden censors where sacred fire is burning—not a false flame kindled by

human passions; and let the heart of the child make
known its requests, assured that the Father's ear is
open. And should that Father have a message of
love, or words of instruction to send by one whose
tongue has caught the accent of angel voices, "let
him speak as the oracles of God;" "and if he minister let him minister as of the ability which God
giveth."

Such is the beautiful ideal which the Friends tried
to realize. And they did realize it to a happy extent; so that Heaven itself seemed to come into their
Meetings, and made them glad with a pure and holy
joy—a joy so deep and sacred that for a time words
were like an intrusion, like obstructions in the sweetly
flowing stream of the Father's love, as it circled about
the fold and the green pastures where the Shepherd
was leading His sheep or watching them as they lay
on the sunny banks. And when He spoke they answered Him, for they knew His voice. Not one only,
but many made answer; for perfect love had cast out
fear, so that even the lambs were not afraid to bleat
in the presence of their mothers and brothers.

Alas, that the time should ever have come when
the voice of the little ones was no longer heard. But
come it did, all too quickly, as the fervor of early
zeal abated, when persecution ceased, and when the
fathers and mothers whom the Lord called with a
baptism of fire had fallen asleep, and children had
taken their places without taking their experiences,

reaping the harvest without sowing the seed—then the atmosphere again became lifeless and cold, and Formalism, which had been banished in her garb of empty words and vain ritual, returned in a ceremony of idle waiting and dead silence.

There is nothing more admirable than the Church of Christ when adorned as a bride for her husband, with all her goodly ornaments, alive in heart and head and hand, her eyes beaming with intelligence and love, even while cast meekly down at her Beloved's feet. A mother of many children will He then call her, and she shall be blessed of them that are ready to perish. But how mournful, on the other hand, is that Church sitting solitary, her children gone from her, her limbs bound with the golden chain which she wore at her bridal, and unwilling that any shall remove it. And the greater the attainment made the greater is the fall when the change comes.

The only possible way to avoid formalism is to *keep alive.* A cemetery will always be a formal place, both when the dead are burying the dead and when silence reigns undisturbed among the graves. Nothing is gained by a do-nothing policy. Action is imperative, and the only escape from wrong action is right action. If we sit down professing to worship God and do it not, how much better are we than those who stand up and make the same profession in vain? But the testimony of the prophet is, "They that wait on the Lord *shall renew their strength ;* they

shall mount up with wings as eagles, they *shall run* and
not be weary, they *shall walk* and not faint." Then if
our waiting fails to bring forth these fruits it is not
waiting *on* the Lord, but waiting *for* the Lord : and
the exchange of one of these prepositions for the other will either build up or ruin any church.

It is very desirable that we should wait on the
Lord in a respectful and proper way : but I would
rather my children should come clamoring around
me, asking for bread and meat three times a day,
than that they should never be hungry enough to ask
for food. Alas for the poor pale lips that never part
in urgent prayer! How the Good Father mourns
over them : and dear Mother Church too often pre-
pares her dainties for them in vain.

We must not be too delicate—not more nice than
wise; and we must always remember that children
have their wants as well as grown people. The inability of the Friends to adapt their system to the
needs of all classes, children as well as adults, un-
reflective minds as well as deep thinkers, has been one
of their greatest deficiencies.

From the nature of the case, silent worship in a
mixed assembly, should not be continued beyond a
moderate length of time. If there are those present
who prefer to meditate longer they should retire,
while the Lord's table is being spread for such as
need tangible food, as these will always be found in
a large majority. And if there is no steward at hand

who is able to "bring out of his treasury things new
and old" adapted to the wants of the needy, tl en
the Church should make haste and "pray the Lord of
the harvest that He will send forth laborers into His
harvest;" and not cease praying until they are sent
in such abundance that there will be found "bread
enough and to spare," wherever the people shall
gather themselves together in the Lord's house.   For
if earthly fathers, when they make a feast for their
children, suffer them not to go away hungry, is it not a
shame that the Father of all should be so misrepre-
sented by His servants as to seem unable to provide
what is good and palatable for all who come to his
house, both young and old, rich and poor, learned
and ignorant.

It is not waiting on God until the Spirit is given
which causes the trouble, but failing to heed the
Spirit and to use the one talent of grace when it is
bestowed.   If we have grace enough to show us
what we need and feel our want, then it is our turn to
act.   "Seek and ye shall find; ask and ye shall receive; knock and it shall be opened unto you."   But
the work too generally stops short, because no one is
found who has confidence enough to go up and knock
manfully at the door of the Lord's treasury.   How
quickly would waiting be turned into joy if such could
always be found: for it is this God desires more
than we desire bread; that He may show Himself
gracious, and feed his little ones to the full, and thus

call them often to His arms. True, it is heart-
knocks only which cause the door to open, and
faith must accompany the blow. But give it gently,
or give it loudly, the Father will hear; and if he do
not answer at once it is because He will try our faith
and teach us to pray more earnestly. That is his way
of drawing us closer to Him.

If we would thus work with God, intelligently,
freely, faithfully, He would lead us on step by step,
until we should soon break out in song—"The Lord
is my shepherd, I shall not want; He maketh me to
lie down in green pastures; He leadeth me beside
the still waters; He restoreth my soul; He leadeth
me in the paths of righteousness for His name's sake."

——"Many are the blessed experiences which I
could relate," says Robert Barclay, "of this silence and
manner of worship; yet I do not so much commend and
speak of this *silence* as if we had bound ourselves by
any law to exclude praying or preaching, or tied ourselves thereunto—not at all; for as our worship con-
sisteth not in words, so neither in silence, as silence,
but *in a holy dependence of the mind upon God;*
from which dependence silence necessarily follows in
the first place, until words can be brought forth which
are from God's Spirit. And God is not wanting to
move in his children to bring forth words of exhortation and prayer when it is needful; so that of the
many gatherings and meetings of such as are con-

vinced of the truth there is scarce any in which God
raiseth not up some or other to minister to his brethren, and there are few meetings that are altogether
silent. For when many are met together in this one
life and name it doth most naturally and frequently
excite them to pray and praise God, and stir up one
another by mutual exhortation and instructions.
Yet we judge it needful that there be in the first place
some time of silence, during which every one may be
gathered inward to the word and gift of grace from
which he that ministereth may receive strength to
bring forth what he ministereth."

Apology—Prop. XI.—§IX.

IV.

"The manifestation of the Spirit is given to every man to profit withal. For to one is given by the Spirit the word of wisdom; to another the word of knowledge by the same Spirit; to another faith by the same Spirit; to another gifts of healing by the same Spirit; to another the working of miracles; to another prophecy; to another discerning of spirits; to another divers kinds of tongues; to another the interpretation of tongues. But all these worketh that one and the selfsame Spirit, dividing to every man severally as He will."—I Cor. XII, 7-11.

Therefore the Friends argue that all preaching of the Gospel should be with inspiration of the Spirit, or, as Paul described his own preaching, "in demonstration of the Spirit and of power."

In every great revival of religion men know that the Spirit dominates them. They feel it as distinctly as they feel the air when the wind is blowing. They cannot see it: they may not be able to analyze its influence, but they know that something besides their own voluntary impulses urges them on. Their souls are invigorated by this mysterious potency, and they

believe in miracles, and do miracles. All at once
they are prophets, and look with unsealed eyes into the
depths of the inner life. They become teachers, ministers, apostles. There is no greater miracle than
this pentecostal outpouring of the spirit in tongues of
fire charged with arrows of conviction for the gathering multitudes. Luther, and every other great re-
former, was an inspired man. He scarcely stopped
to consider it, but worked on, like Vulcan at
his forge, and hammered out the thunderbolts of
the Reformation. Could he have done this without the breath and fire of Heaven blowing and
burning all around and within him? George Fox
was a man of the same class, though of a different
temper. He was like John as compared with Peter;
but he too was a "son of thunder," notwithstanding
his peaceful and loving disposition. He saw more
distinctly than Luther what agencies were accom-
plishing the work to which he was called. He lay on
the Master's breast, and could look up and ask Him
questions. Thus he set the type for his followers,
and became the founder of a new school of prophets.
Penn and Barclay preached and wrote, Burrough and
Naylor proclaimed the Gospel with power as they were
moved by the Spirit. No doubt some chaff, and perhaps
a little cockle was contained in the handfuls of wheat
they threw out; but the Lord's truth was there in
such abundance that the fields soon became green,
and the sweet rustling of the tender leaves could be

] eard on every side, as the spirit breathed upon them.

The theory of Friends is that preaching should be attempted only when the presence of the Spirit is *felt*; otherwise silence should be maintained even if nothing be done in a meeting but to sit together and meditate.

But granting the truth of the proposition that without the Spirit's aid no service can be performed acceptably to God, several important questions arise as to the degree of inspiration requisite for a beginning and for continuance;—whether this aid is always consciously bestowed or may sometimes be unconsciously possessed; and whether the fruits of a previous inspiration may not be appropriately brought forward to supply a deficiency in the present amount of spiritual rain-fall.

Suppose we had no water for use but such as falls every day! An enthusiast might say to us that God will supply us daily with whatever we need, as He did the Israelites in the wilderness, when manna fell every morning, and when water from the rock followed them in their journeys, and the cloud directed their course. There are doubtless times when such care is to be expected. It was needful for Israel in the wilderness during the transition period, but it was not continued in the land of Canaan. There they lived a short time on the spontaneous fruits of the land, and then went to raising wheat, and planting vineyards. So in the highest system of Providence, the labor of man unites with the gifts of heaven to en-

large and preserve them and make the supply uniform.

We ought indeed to "covet earnestly the best gifts,"
and there is no doubt that prophesying, or speaking
from the spirit directly, is the more satisfactory mode
of preaching the Gospel, and far the most effective,
as Paul showed—far more than speaking in an un-
known tongue.   Yet the apostle did both, and much
besides.   He made himself all things to all men.   His
object was to win souls to Christ, not to defend a
theory: and so, like his Master, he used every means
that came within his reach to convert men and build
them up in the truth.   When one method failed, he
tried another.   We preached, prayed, prophesied,
talked in various languages, in season and out of season, like a fountain that runs at all times, whether
you want the water or not; wrote letters, worked with
his hands and went on missionary expeditions; cir-
cumcised his converts and refused circumcision; ate
meat and refused meat; exhorted, remonstrated,
scolded, wept; sang hymns and discoursed on theology; healed the sick and raised the dead.   Thus he
became the great, broad, efficient builder of many
churches, and the best single representative of Christ's
fullness which the world has known.   Such a man,
saturated all through with the inspiration of Divine
life and love, is surely a better model for the Christian minister than any which our fragmentary wisdom
has presented to the modern church.

What the church wants is not less inspiration, but more. We want an inspiration which will affect us not merely once or twice in a week, but which will remain with us, showing its fruits in every-day word and action. We want inspired writing, inspired conversation, inspired teaching of the young, inspired reading, inspired hand-shaking, inspired praying and singing, inspired essays on subjects of vital interest to ourselves and others. In short, inspiration should run all through the church, filling it with life and warmth, and then we should have preaching that would be inspired indeed—filled with the love, wisdom, tenderness and zeal of Christ, and with His healing power to recover the sick, and break the bondage of sin. Oh, that we might once more witness the fullness of such an inspiration as moved the saints of old, and which wrought liberty and enlargement in Zion.

The question of inspiration is necessarily an obscure one. "The wind bloweth where it listeth, and thou hearest the sound thereof but canst not tell whence it cometh or whither it goeth." It is God's prerogative to work in secret and come to our aid when and where He pleases. All are not sensitive alike to spiritual impressions, nor is the same degree of persuasion required to guide or set the minds of all in action. A slight touch of the rein will keep a well trained horse in the path chosen by his master, while a strong pull is needed for one of stubborn will. Moreover, as our religious life and experience enlarge we are enabled to retain the instructions imparted by the Spirit for a longer time, and to co-operate with God in a more uniform way, so as to be able, at length, to teach divine truths with regularity and at the same time with force and unction.

Never, indeed, should we be found working wholly without God—without that realizing sense which the Spirit gives of the truths we utter. So far the Friends are clearly right, as opposed to any who attempt to labor in "the night, when no man can work" effectively. But there is every shade of twilight, from the faint glimmer of early dawn to sunrise; and work is not all wasted that is done between the two.

As the time seems fast approaching when we shall, in a sense, have "no night," in favored places on this earth, whose bowels flow with oil, and whose air is an ocean of electric fire, so when the Church realizes the ideal of its Founder and becomes as a city set on a hill, whose glory shines afar, day without night, or as a "woman clothed with the sun," then our "whole body shall be full of light," and our power for effectual working will not be intermittent as at first.

True it is that for many a long day of our school life God will need to show us that we are dealing with something quite different from the spirit of subject Nature which we can harness to our car at our own will. Often He will quench our glory behind clouds which our hand is not strong enough to remove, until we learn the great lesson that "it is God that worketh in us both to will and to do *of His own good pleasure;*" and that therefore we must work "with trembling," while the light shines. And yet "the path of the righteous is as the shining light that shineth brighter and brighter unto the perfect day."

Two dangers lie very near those who believe in special inspiration. One is the danger of mistaking lamplight for sunlight. The other that of thinking sunlight sufficient without any aid from lamplight. Many a minister sets fire regularly to his dim, smoky candle, or his lamp filled with old oil, in the day time, supposing that he is really bringing fresh light from heaven to his drowsy hearers. Others, on the contrary, refuse to light their lamps, even in the night; and would have a minister of Christ like a room with only sky-lights and no side windows to let in reflected light from nature and human literature. Now a minister of the Gospel without a glass dome over his head, or so much as one small window, is a pitiable object; but at the same time "whatsoever doth make manifest is light," and the power of genuine inspiration is greatly enlarged when the mind wrought upon is furnished with suitable material for the Spirit's use.

V.

When Friends adopted the principle of absolute sincerity and truthfulness in worship, it struck at the root of many customs. Among these was formal prayer. Prayer is essentially formal when uninspired, or unaccompanied by active desires corresponding with the words used, whether these words be read, rehearsed from memory, or extemporized by the intellect. All such utterances fall below the highest Christian standard, even when made under a sense of duty by Christian people. They belong to that large class of idle words for which the perfect Judge will call us to account as we come to see that God is a God of truth, and requires of all His children "truth in the inward parts."

But here we come again upon the constantly recurring question, What shall people do who are *not* perfect? who are learning how to put words and things, sound and sense, together? Will God hold such to strict account for every sentence which tells Him how we know we ought to feel, though our poor laggard hearts refuse to respond with dutiful sentiments? What if our prayers are like wheat heads only half filled with grain, and the rest pretentious chaff, will He throw them all away? Or will He take what wheat there is and blow away the chaff with His kindly breath? Shall we raise no wheat till we can present a good full crop of forty bushels to the acre? Shall we put up no prayers until every word can come before God laden with throbbing emotions and desires? Manifestly this is not good husbandry. It is not the way we treat our children. We do not expect perfection from them. We bear with their weaknesses, and do not hush their voices when, with "lisping, stammering tongue," they are learning how to talk. And yet as they advance we endeavor to hold them more and more closely to the demands of good sense and absolute truthfulness.

Here is where the Quaker system so often proved impracticable, because it was designed for a state of society far in advance of the world's attainment when it was introduced. In a select company, gathered amid the fires of persecution and bound in closest fellowship thereby, it worked admirably; but as chastened human nature began to re-assert itself in the next and succeeding generations, the ideal standard was found so far in advance of the comfortable body of its followers that in trying to regulate their conduct by it they were like a factory built to run by steam but situated so far from the engine room that the steam cools before it reaches the works. A good water power, with all its waste of energy, and its splashing of waters, will do more execution than such a steam power as that.

The result was that public prayer became less and less frequent, until in many meetings it came to be of rare occurrence. They accepted, as if for all occasions, the Lord's injunction to private prayer: "But thou when thou prayest enter into thy closet and shut the door: there pray to thy Father in secret; and thy Father who seeth in secret shall reward thee openly." The heart being taken for the closet, the rule was thus extended to the public assembly where each was to pray in secret for the things needed. All this was very beautiful and apt, had it not stopped short of the *open reward*. The proper result of a company of Christians all praying together in secret is that a flame will break out from the burning coals and lift itself toward heaven with such glowing warmth of utterance that all hearts will rejoice together with that consummate joy which is to be found only in the fit expression of the soul's emotions. For, talk as we may about silence being "golden" and speech "silvern," the old proverb is nearer the truth, that "words fitly spoken are as apples of gold in pictures of silver." The crown of all joy is its happy expression; and too often for the want of the "word in season" a prosperous Quaker meeting has exchanged the silence of sweet meditation for the silence of death. The fruits of God's love may dwell a long time in the womb of the soul, but sooner or later they must achieve ex-

pression or death follows. Many a poor heart knows
this to be true from travail that has brought it
almost to the grave. Then yielding, it has found,
by a few words submissively spoken, the joy of the
ransomed at the gates of Heaven.

In this way God has long brought forth His children in the ministry by the cross of Christ, and so
long as enough of these are born into the Church she
will prosper, but when, for any cause, they fail to appear, the song of the reapers will cease.

Ministers in the Society of Friends have often been
greatly at fault in this matter, from an overwrought
niceness which increases by indulgence until power
and facility in prayer are lost, or rather are never
gained, from slight use of the gift, which like all other gifts requires cultivation. Waiting for a com-
manding impulse, or seduced by the theory that private prayer is sufficient, the minister fails to voice
the common need and gather the spirits of the people
into that unity of desire and purpose which is the
key to Heaven's richest blessings. Jesus laid great
stress on unity in prayer, pledging His Father's
blessing if any two of His disciples should be agreed
as touching any thing they would ask in His name.
The most natural way to effect such agreement is by
a hearty expression of what one earnest mind feels,
thus calling forth the "amen" which clasps all hearts
in one. The elements of right emotions and desires
lie dormant in many souls, waiting to be gathered

into form by a happy utterance, and just as we all become poets when a poet speaks, many are made supplicants by one earnest pleader. This is the sacred office of him whose heart is fired and whose lips are moved by the Holy Ghost. And blessed is he whose thoughts and words are thus formed into a ladder reaching from earth to Heaven, whereon the angels of God may be seen ascending and descending with blessings for the children of men.

VI.

SINGING AND MUSIC.

The delicate Quaker conscience was not long in discovering that singing psalms and hymns in concert, by a mixed company of believers and unbelievers, with musical accompaniment, opened the door to grave perversions of the truth, and often reduced a serious, and what should be a sacred act, to a merely sensuous entertainment. They did not condemn singing in itself as necessarily wrong. Indeed, during the first warm days of the new spring-tide, before the Society had grown formal, exercised minds often broke out in "psalms and hymns and spiritual songs," giving praise to the Lord of Hosts whose arm was wondrously made bare for the triumph of his cause and the deliverance of his oppressed people. It is probable, though not certain, that those who were familiar with the metrical hymns of the day, sometimes used these as the vehicle of their devotional sentiments. Others improvised both the words and music and thus originated that peculiar style of intoning parts of their sermons which so long characterized the majority of their speakers; but which finally came under censure as the society grew more cultured and less enthusiastic.

When and how the use of singing as a part of worship was discontinued is not recorded. It was probably a gradual result of the prevailing tendency to seriousness and ethical refinement—a growing sensitiveness to whatever was felt to be incongruous with the general spirit of the meetings. But even before this, music as an art had fallen under ban and was forbidden to Friends under pain of disowment. It is not until quite recently that a reaction has taken place, finally making the law a dead letter. The struggle was a long and painful one, causing many a heartache, and frequent ruptures of social relations, as member after member was divided from the body for the *sin* of allowing music to be taught and practiced in his family. But now it is very common.

In the extreme van of the "orthodox" branch of the Society hymn singing is again cautiously making its appearance. It began with individual voices; but slowly others gained courage to join, until at length hymn books have been issued, and children in the "First-day schools" are in some cases taught to sing in concert. This is probably the entering wedge to its final adoption as a part of social worship, and then will arise the danger of the pendulum again swinging to the opposite extreme. Happy will it be for Friends if they can preserve the true medium in this as well as other departments of religion.

It ought not to need argument to prove to any intelligent mind that a propensity of our nature which

God has made so strong that no amount of oppression
can crush it out should have room for rational religious exercise. A happy child sings as naturally as a
lark. From first to last the Bible overflows with
proofs that singing and music are the native wings of
praise. Whenever the Spirit of God has powerfully
pervaded the soul of man it has risen spontaneously
in adoring songs, and if capable of doing so has accompanied the words with melodious sounds, either
vocal or instrumental, or both.

The only practical question which presents any
difficulty is that of regulating the exercise in a way
to prevent abuse. The moment truth and sincerity
are sacrificed to sound, Religion cries out in pain, and
the angels fly away. Not unfrequently the devil
comes in their place and sets the people to criticising
the performance as a work of art, or carries them
quite away from all devotional engagements in admiration of pleasant sounds. When the followers of
Jesus thus turn from Him who sang with His disciples, but not, we may be sure, to please the ear
of man, and worship at the shrine of Polyhymnia,
it is time to reflect on those words of strong warning,
"If thy right eye cause thee to offend pluck it out
and cast it from thee, for it is better for thee to enter
into life with one eye than having two eyes to be cast
into Gehenna." It was probably on this principle
that the Friends excluded hymn-singing from their
worship, and unless it can be con lucted with a reas_

onable degree of worshipful sentiment and truthfulness they are certainly right in rejecting it wholly. Much of our fashionable church music must be a blasphemous discord in the ears of God, when hired artists take in their unhallowed lips words meet only for angels or blood-washed saints, while the people sit like children, their thoughts dissipated and carried about on waves of meaningless sound. There is urgent need of reform in this matter.

And yet it is an over-nice demand of conscience which forbids our ever using words that do not exactly represent our own feelings and experiences. To some extent we may properly personate the writer of a hymn in singing, as we do in reading. Our minds and feelings may enter into the words uttered as far as they are able, and by thus bringing pious thoughts into view our hearts may be sympathetically affected and drawn out in worship, when otherwise they would have remained inactive. This is a legitimate effect of singing, as well as reading; and sentiments may be brought closer to us by our taking good words representatively on our lips, than by hearing others speak them. Conviction is sometimes wrought in this way by the Spirit. Properly guarded against abuses the influence for good thus exerted by sacred songs is of great value, and is one of the agencies most available for purifying and deepening the fountains of youthful aspiration. To say nothing of the proper attractions thus given to the place of worship, these high and holy uses commend Christian singing as almost equal in efficiency to the other two arms of Divine service—preaching and prayer.

It may be difficult to bring congregational singing properly under control of the Spirit, and yet it ought not to be impossible. The Spirit of God is the Spirit of love, wisdom and a sound mind. It always acts rationally as well as with fervor, and is not averse to order and regularity. And the human heart and mind, however changeful in some of their moods, ought to gain stability of purpose so that devotional sentiments of various kinds may be in constant, though perhaps latent, possession. This is really the case. The soul of a mature Christian is not like a frail anemone whose blossoms come forth in the spring and do not appear again in a twelvemonth; but rather it is like an orange grove in the south, blossoming and bearing fruit at all seasons. And there should be enough of these in every Christian assembly to respond to the invitation to sing our Father's worthy praise, or utter forth the longings and aspirations of inspired poets with honest enthusiasm. Is it not a part of the church's business to educate all, and especially the young, so that they may unite, as they feel inclined, in these acts of social worship. In this way many a heart would be enabled to give utterance to its feelings, which would do so in no other way, and through even so humble a participation in the vocal service, to find comfort and strength.

——"As to the singing of psalms," says Barclay, " there will not be need of any long discourse : for that the case is just the same as in the two former of preaching and prayer. We confess this to be a part of God's worship ; and very sweet and refreshing when it proceeds from a true sense of God's love in the heart, and arises from a divine influence of the Spirit that leads souls to breathe forth either a sweet harmony, or words suitable to the present condition, whether they be words formerly used by the saints and recorded in Scripture, such as the Psalms of David, or other words ; as were the hymns and songs of Zacharias, Simeon, and the blessed Virgin Mary. But as for the formal customary way of singing, it hath no foundation in Scripture, nor any ground in Christianity : yea besides all the abuses incident to prayer and preaching it hath this more peculiar, that oftentimes great and horrid lies are said in the sight of God : for all manner of wicked and profane people take upon them to personate the experiences and conditions of the blessed David which are not only false as to them, but also as to some of more sobriety who utter them forth."

Apology, Prop. XI, §XXVI.

VII.

The vital force, no less than the distinguishing grace of the Christian religion, lies in that Divine love which prompted Jesus to labor, suffer and die for the benefit of mankind, looking for no other reward than that which a father finds in the safety and happiness of his children. Whatever does not partake of this spirit is foreign to the Gospel of Christ. It is obvious, therefore, that the Christian Ministry must rest on this lofty foundation, or sink to the lower plane of worldly avocations; and perhaps the worst effect of making it a salaried office, is that it has a tendency to degrade the sacred calling to a level with secular professions, and thus rob it of the glory of a Divine mission. No other proof of this tendency is needed than the fact that it so stands in the popular estimate, being classed as one of the three learned professions, with law and medicine; and this without a protest from the "legates of the skies." The consequences are, that not only is the office secularized in the common estimation, but a vast amount of hypocrisy and selfishness become mixed up with the ministry of the Gospel, through temptations offered to unsanctified men to make it a road to honor and comfort, instead of the thorny path of self-denial which Christ and his apostles found it.

George Fox and his friends clearly saw this great evil and set their faces against it with the zeal of true reformers. They had ample opportunity to realize the baleful effects of making the priesthood a mercenary office; for veritable wolves in sheep's clothing, paid by State, or with tithes cruelly wrung from the poor, and from unwilling dissenters, drove them from their homes to starve in prison, until "hireling priest" became in their minds a synonym for Anti-Christ. Well might they ask, and well may we, even now, consider, what it was that so transformed the followers of Him who came to save and uplift the lowly by putting Himself as a trodden stone beneath their feet. Was it not simply the fact that in course of time, as Christianity became popular, the ministry was allowed to degenerate into a lucrative office? From this "root of all evil" have grown up the enormous perversions that so often in the past have rendered Christ's professed servants a hissing and a by-word among those whom they oppressed. And while it is easy for us now to say that these evils came from the abuse of a just privilege, would it not be well to examine very closely the fountain which has sent forth such a stream, in order that we may find exactly how and where the corruption entered?

Jesus laid the governing principle of his ministers'

labor and support in the law of reciprocal love, so succinctly stated in the directions He gave to his disciples when first sending them forth to proclaim the Gospel. What are His words? "As ye go preach, saying, The Kingdom of Heaven is at hand. Heal the sick, raise the dead, cleanse the lepers, cast out devils : freely ye have received, freely give. Provide neither gold nor silver nor brass in your purses ; no wallet for your journey, neither two coats nor shoes, nor staff: for the laborer is worthy of his food."—Matt. X, 7-10. What are the points of duty thus authoritatively laid down ?

First, Preach the Gospel and do good wherever you go, freely, heartily, lovingly, as Christ has taught and done good to you.

Second, As Christ's servants, look to Him for support : neither provide for yourselves, as though the work were your own, nor exact aid from men ; but accept the contributions of such as will give freely, as the proper fruit of your ministry.

How evident it is, from the simple statement of this supremely wise law, that had the Christian Ministry always literally obeyed its injunctions there would never have arisen so much as one of the bitter complaints that have marked the advent of the Church to popularity and power. The neglect to maintain Christ's ordinance precisely as He established it has caused all the disgrace and mischief.

The corruption grew up very gradually, as all such

evils do, from slight deviations at the beginning,
these being soon enlarged by their own bad effects
until a new and entirely opposite principle was established, and the Gospel of free salvation was transformed into an engine of tyranny and extortion.

Two false ideas lie at the root of this corrupt
growth. The first is, that Christ's ministers have a
right to use the power which their position gives
them to *exact* compensation from the people for what
they do for them.

The second is, that the people have a right to use
the property in their possession as owners, and not
as the Lord's stewards.

Eradicate these two errors from the minds of all
Christians and the silver railing which Mammon has
built around the sanctuary in the Temple of God will
disappear.

To banish the first error wholly from His disciples'
minds Christ poured His own Spirit upon them at
Pentacost, and often afterwards, as they needed. And
to exclude the latter, He moved them voluntarily to
surrender all their property for the common use, and
punished with death some whose half-hearted devotion made them liars against the Holy Ghost.

Probably the two errors grew up together, as
it is certain that they now stimulate and sustain
each other,—like Beelzebub and Mammon, working in nether darkness to build a Pandemonium
under the Church : and many a Church has fallen

into spiritual ruin through their devices. As the
number of converts increased and the atmosphere
grew less electrical with the conscious presence of the
Spirit, and the expectation of Christ's personal return, the great miracle of full-souled consecration of
heart and tongue and purse to the self-rewarding
service of love became less and less conspicuous.
Finding that no more Ananiases were stricken down,
lukewarm Christians began to retain half—two-
thirds — three-fourths — ninety-nine-hundredths of
their property for their personal use and convenience,
while the more zealous servants of Christ went poorly clad and ill fed on their journeys. At other times
some avaricious Bishop began to embezzle the common property of the Church for himself and his
favorites, until prudent laymen found it advisable to
retain portions of their earnings in their own title.
In this way the change was at length established
which divided the property of Christians into
Church property, and private property, the latter
transferable only at the will of the holders, the
former to be used in the discretion of appointed
trustees or bishops. This is no doubt the only
practical system in the present state of society;
but no change of social conditions can alter the law
of Christ as a spiritual bond between himself and his
disciples. By this law the entire property of Christians is subject to his order for the interests of his
kingdom, and to refuse what those interests call for

is rebellion against Him who claims not only our property but ourselves, as absolutely his : for "we are not
our own, we are bought with a price :" and that price
an infinite one. Who then shall dare refuse what
the King of Kings demands? especially when those
demands are prompted by purest love for those on
whom they are made? And yet thousands do refuse, and hold tenaciously to what is not theirs ; and
this incites the needy pastor, when the claims of love
and duty are found insufficient, to appeal to the
meaner motives by which men of the world are
moved, and instead of giving the gospel freely, to condition his preaching on legal guaranties of support.
The temptation to do this is exceedingly great, if a
minister has a family dependent upon him; and the
motive may be entirely unselfish, aiming at securing
his just rights in what seems to many the only practicable way. And yet, simple and reasonable as the
act appears from the prudential standpoint, it is a
breach of faith, a rejection of Christ's order, and a
holding of the grace of God for sale. "My Kingdom
is not of this world," said Jesus ; and whoever appeals to the powers of this world to secure his rights
as a citizen of Christ's kingdom is plainly acting the
the part of an alien.

Even to ask a pledge that the Church will faithfully perform its duty, is like requiring an oath of a
Christian. It is a reproach to that sacred name which
alone ought to contain the highest pledge of veracity

and honor. But experience has too often shown
that double incentives to faithfulness are sometimes
needed by that large class of Christians who, while
spending nearly their whole time and energies in
promoting their interests in this world, with means
at command, leave those who would gladly work for
the Master in higher fields so poorly provided, that
little advancement can be made, while millions are
starving for the light which a few easily-spared dol-
lars from each well-provided member of Christ's flock
would send them. How long shall the Savior of
mankind stretch forth his streaming hands and bid
us look on Him whom *we* have pierced.

From the foregoing I make these inferences :—

First, However convenient or excusable, in view of
the neglect of churches to make suitable provision
for the ministry without such constraint, the contract
system, in all its forms, is wrong in method, and often
wrong in spirit, being a plain infringement of an order of Christ which is in harmony with the whole
scheme of the Gospel.

Second, The term "salary," or "pay," applied to
what is assigned to a minister, is objectionable; because a salary is compensation for service done, and
the ministry of the gospel, if it proceeds from the
love of God, cannot be thus compensated. The term
" allowance," as sometimes used in this connection,
is preferable: for a minister's support, or "food," is
what is allowed him, out of the common stores to live

upon while doing the work to which the Master calls
him. The allowance may be uniform and liberal, if
means are sufficient, and it is the plain duty of the
Church to secure such a distribution of its resources
as will be productive of the best result for all concerned.

Third, Brotherly love, and gratitude to God for the
benefits of the gospel, should prompt all to use their
entrusted talents, of whatever kind, for mutual blessing, and the furtherance of the good work. That the
people are left free to appropriate the means in their
command makes them directly responsible to Christ
himself, who, as the final Judge, has declared that
he will requite any neglect shown to his brethren as
shown to himself personally. "Inasmuch as ye *did*
it not to one of these, my brethren, ye did it not to
me". If such considerations are not sufficient, the
messenger should shake the dust from his feet, and
find a less thorny and rocky soil in which to sow his
seed. Or if the people are poor he should help with
his hands.

Fourth, Ministers ought not to decline offerings
properly tendered, but should avail themselves of the
natural and right fruits of Christian love and kindness,
to extend the benefits of the gospel to the utmost;
and when the people are selfish or negligent they
should exhort and stimulate them by all proper
means to the discharge of so responsible a duty. If
then our motives and conduct be upright this will

generally be found sufficient without resort to measures of a doubtful kind.

The arguments and illustrations of the apostle
Paul accord fully, and are evidently based upon the
ordinance of Christ, made when He first sent out his
disciples to preach. In the ninth chapter of I Corinthians Paul says: "What soldier ever serveth at
his own charges? who planteth a vineyard and eateth
not the fruit thereof? or who feedeth a flock and eateth not of the milk of the flock? . . . 'Thou
shalt not muzzle the ox when he treadeth out the
corn.' . . . If we sowed into you in spiritual
things is it a great matter if we shall reap your carnal things? Nevertheless we did not use this right;
but we bear all things that we may cause no hindrance to the gospel of Christ. Know ye not that
they which minister about sacred things eat of the
things of the temple, and they which wait upon the
altar have their portion with the altar? Even so did
the Lord ordain that they which proclaim the gospel
should live of the gospel."

The right order is thus distinctly reiterated, to the
exclusion of all bargaining, or resort to force, on the
one hand, and all independency on the other, except
as circumstances make it expedient to sacrifice a natural right where more good may be done by acts of
self-denial. Such was often the apostle's case, and
has been that of thousands of ministers of all denom-

inations, in times of trial. But though all should
strive manfully and endure hardship as good soldiers
in times of depression, after the victory has been
measurably gained, all should enjoy the fruits of
peace together, and enter upon a more orderly system
of husbandry, each laborer performing the part for
which he is best qualified, and receiving a just share
of all the fruits of the combined industry. This is all
that is intended in the common practice of assigning
a certain sum (called a salary or allowance) to the
use of ministers or other officers in the church. Of
course where nothing is needed nothing should be received for one's own use; but whatever is freely offered should be devoted to the service where need
exists. A man who employs his superior gifts to gain
money for private indulgence while his poorer brethren suffer, is the meanest kind of a hireling. And the
minister who can labor, with brain or hands, to supply his necessities, without injury to his service, is
bound to do so. The second of the two great commandments should be the governing law in this
whole matter—"Thou shalt love thy neighbor as
thyself."

In bearing a vigorous testimony against the cor-
ruptions of a man-made and state-paid ministry the
Friends were almost inevitably carried to an opposite extreme. They considered, and perhaps rightly, that they were acting in one of those crises in
which the man of God must take his life in his hand,

and freely give his all to the support of a great reform. In this view they were justified in imitating
Paul's example, that the power of true religion might
be again conspicuously illustrated. The first fruits
were no doubt wholesome and satisfactory; but as
in other things, having begun to go in an opposite
direction to the practices of the times they knew not
how to stop; and so they were gradually carried on
to an impracticable point. While enthusiasm ran
high their self-supporting ministry was well sustained
by new recruits; but as the fires of early zeal abated
men were not so readily found, who were willing to act
as missionaries, and go long journeys, leaving their
families in want, or to be cared for as indigent
members of the Society. Thus by neglecting to en-
courage and support a free and active ministry, lest
their testimony against a "hireling ministry" should be
weakened, they crippled the service, and rendered it
less efficient from the want of cultivated talent, time not
being given their ministers to improve their minds and
exercise their gifts to the best advantage. At the same
time the people, many of whom soon became prosperous and wealthy by their frugal and industrious
modes of living, were deprived of that training to lib-
erality which the habit of generous giving bestows.

Perhaps it is needless to pursue the subject further, as my aim is not to say all that can, fittingly,
be said, but to bring into view, as clearly and briefly
as possible, the fundamental principles of Christian

economy, leaving the application to those who understand the particular circumstances of individuals or of societies.

Great credit is certainly due to the Quaker Ministry for the zeal, fidelity and devotion with which they have always done their work, many of them traveling vast distances, and making frequent visits, to water and refresh the languishing vineyard, in the purest "springs of gospel affection," without a momentary desire for aught in return but that "peace which passeth understanding." And this they received from that appreciative Master who knows how to reward his servants with something infinitely better than silver and gold. Indeed the man who can look upon such things as a *reward* for saving immortal souls is worthy of the disdain which every honest Quaker feels for the sheep-tender who "fleeth because he is a hireling and careth not for the sheep."

To show that the views here expressed are in substantial agreement with those of early Friends I again quote from their accepted exponent.

——"They who have received this holy and unspotted gift, *as they have freely received it so are they freely to give it*, without hire or bargaining, far less to use it as a *Trade* to get money by: yet if God has called any from their employment or trades by which they acquire their livelihood, it may be lawful for such, according to the liberty which they feel given them in the Lord, to receive such temporals (to wit, what may be needed for them for meat and clothing) as are given them freely and cordially by those to whom they have communicated spirituals."

Apology, Prop. X.

" We freely acknowledge, as the *proposition* holds forth, that there is an obligation upon such to whom God sends, or among whom he raiseth up a minister, that, if need be, they minister to his necessities. Secondly, That it is lawful for him to receive what is necessary and convenient . . . . . That which we then oppose in this matter is, First that it should be constrained and limited : Secondly, that it should be superfluous, chargeable, and sumptuous."

Barclay's Apology, etc.

VIII.

UNIVERSAL BROTHERHOOD.

Few have maintained the doctrine of the Universal Brotherhood of Mankind as thoroughly, and constantly, as the Friends. It springs naturally from their assertion of the universal efficacy of Christ's offering, through the world-wide ministry of the Spirit, whereby a seed of Divine life is again implanted in every soul, and nourished by "that light which lighteth every man that cometh into the world". All men, being thus reinstated in the covenant of life are again made brethren. There is neither pagan nor alien, except as sin, or voluntary refusal to accept the offered grace, which would bring forth a holy life, if united with and obeyed, makes heathen, or enemies of God, alike in "Christian" and "Pagan" countries. Hence wherever Friends traveled they felt bound to recognize all men as on a level in the sight of God, and to look for the signs of that spiritual birth which, through the Second Adam, has "of one blood made all nations to dwell on the face of the earth."

It was this broad view of Christianity, together with its genuine spirit in their hearts, which led them to treat the American Indians with such uniform kind-

ness and justice as almost to prove their doctrine, that
the wildest savage has a latent germ of heavenly life
within him awaiting only the heart's consent, or the
breath of love from souls already enkindled to active
virtue, to bring forth the image of Christ. The one
bright thread running through the dark history of
European settlements in America is the steadfast and
almost romantic friendship which grew up between
the Quakers and Indians, and which has outlasted
every change down to the present day. The unhappy
foresters, hunted like wolves by the avaricious inva-
der, and insufficiently protected in their rights by
other colonists, and by the Government of a great nation, have never lacked an advocate in the successors
of Penn, and have never failed to appreciate the kindness and reciprocate it when opportunity offered.
No Quaker has ever knowingly been killed by an Indian. This episode in the great tragedy by which
a vast continent has been almost depopulated of its
native inhabitants is of itself sufficient to immortalize
the name of Friends.

They have been equally true to the oppressed Af-
ricans as their duty has been made apparent, having
been the first to abolish slavery in their own Society—
in many instances paying the emancipated blacks for
their past services—and thenceforward heading the
moral opposition to the system. They always aided
the poor fugitives in their efforts to escape from
bondage, and though they could not sanction the use

of the sword, none rejoiced more heartily in the final overthrow of this enormous wrong to humanity.

All other humanitarian interests have met from them a similar response, especially the great causes of Peace and Temperance ; and though they have hitherto generally shrunk from politics, through fear of incurring responsibility for what they conceived to be the unchristian acts of Government, they are uniformly to be found on the side of equal rights for all.

Friends have not entered largely into Missionary work, but are beginning to retrieve this error in some parts of the Society. They have probably been hindered in this great Christian enterprise for the conversion of the world by their theory of the Universal Light of Christ—deeming this sufficient for the honestly disposed, without the external aids of history and a preached gospel. It is common to hear the remark among them that we have plenty of heathen in what are called Christian countries, and that we need not go abroad for them. This is a truism, and yet the outward knowledge of Christianity, though not absolutely necessary to salvation, is profitable for religious growth and development ; and probably in a great majority of cases it is the stimulating cause of the first conception of religion in the soul. It is like water and sunlight to vegetable germs. Without these they would ever lie dormant, or make but an ineffectual beginning. Without the concentrated light which the historic knowledge of Christianity gives, the secret germs of virtue, which are indeed, like certain vegetable germs, found floating in the atmosphere of all countries, will fail to generate moral and spiritual life. What little does germinate in the dim twilight of pagan traditions is usually poor and feeble, like arctic shrubbery. Knowledge is the incubating mother of all the virtues, and though vice often flourishes under its beams, like weeds in a rank and badly cultivated soil, still it is true that most of the advanced growths of humanity are to be found in Christian lands. None of us would wish our children reared where the light of the historic Gospel is not visibly shining. Therefore, as much as in us lies, we ought to aid in scattering its beams in all places, near and remote, helping on the time when "the knowledge of the Lord shall cover the earth as the waters cover the sea."

IX.

EQUALITY OF WOMAN.

The equal right and duty of woman to labor in all
departments of the Gospel with man, and especially
among her own sex, has been from the first a distinguishing doctrine of the Friends. And it is one that
does honor to their discernment and freedom from
the bias of custom and tradition. There is no surer
index to the advancement of civilization than the ele-
vation of woman to her natural and appropriate place
in society.

If you would learn what that place is make your
home in a well-disposed and cultured Christian family, where sons and daughters grow up from infancy
together in the free atmosphere of hallowed domestic
love. Whatever natural differences you note there
may be presumed to belong to the original plan.
But what do you discover? Any broad distinctions
of sex in the intellectual and moral developments of
home life? Do the boys do all the talking, and teaching, and preaching, and law making, carried on in that
model republic? I am tempted to let one of the boys,
who has gained some recent masculine accomplish-
ments in the street, answer " *You bet* they don't."

And yet everything goes on as it should in nature's primary training-school, where all are teachers and all scholars, all preachers and all hearers, by turns.

Now the Church of Christ should be such a Christian home enlarged and specially devoted to the cultivation of religion and morals, with this addition, that, as an adult force in the world, the Church is to carry forward an aggressive work of evangelization and reform into regions more or less hostile to its doctrine and spirit. Whatever adaptations of its working energy this condition of things requires ought to be made with a view mainly to efficience in realizing the objects sought. Where men prove to be abler expounders of the truth, better teachers, more impressive exhorters, they should be put forward to do the work for which they are best qualified. The same may be affirmed on the other hand of women. The doctrine of equal rights must be held with a proper regard to the ends in view. Neither man nor woman has any right to impede the progress of truth. If we cannot help we should not hinder.

The enforcement of this rule of expediency has, from various causes in the past, devolved the public services of the church mostly on the male sex. But it is obvious that the growth of society may largely modify this arrangement and bring woman more and more to the front, until, in the good time coming, as in the olden Paradise, she will stand side by side with man in the congenial labors and heav-

enly joys of that Eden which is to encompass the
world.

Such is the beautiful vision offered to us by that
Savior who consented to be born of woman that he
might undo the fruit of Eve's untimely ambition.
For, if the bad ambition of our first mother to gain
unlawful knowledge and lead her husband to higher
wisdom, caused her to be put under his governance
for a time, surely the meekness and faith of Mary,
second Eve, should restore her daughters in faith to
all the primeval privileges and rank.   That such was
God's purpose appears highly credible when we consider the respect and love shown to pious women in
the early church where the right to prophesy, or
speak from the Spirit, was never denied her. This
undoubted fact settles the whole question as to
woman's right, under the Gospel, to obey the
impulses of the Holy Spirit. To go beyond this
and talk foolishly, or "gabble," as Paul expressed it
in speaking of the Corinthian women, is lawful for
neither woman nor man.   The right is sometimes ar-
rogated by the male sex, but there is one law for all
in the presence-chamber of the King of Saints, and
that law is to speak what the Master bids; or, which
is often the same thing, what love, intelligence and
good sense clearly dictate.   No one respected the
just rights of women more than did the Apostle Paul
who several times in his epistles makes mention of
their ministry in terms which imply, if not full equal-

ity with men, at least the rank of co-laborers. The restrictive language which he uses at certain times must, by the necessary laws of interpretation, be understood in the light of his known practice. When he says "Let your women keep silence in the churches, for it is not permitted unto them to speak," or *talk lightly*, as the Greek word signifies, we refer back to his directions in the same letter how women shall be attired when they pray or prophesy in public, and the meaning is plain. Women must have a covering of the Spirit, symbolized by a veil, or long hair, in order to justify her in assuming to minister to man who is her natural head. This Divine warrant protects her from the authority of man, or the "angels" that govern the churches, and in that liberty she can do aught that will edify the body. But without that unction which made Deborah a judge, and Anna a prophetess, she is an intruder in the mixed public assembly. Her speech, not being "seasoned with grace," becomes mere "*gabbling*" and is forbidden by the laws of common propriety. This covers the entire principle of woman's ministry. Among her own sex she has the same liberty that man enjoys among his brethren, and may speak freely of secondary matters without special inspiration. This is why the Friends divided their business meetings so that women might confer together about what concerned the welfare and good order of their part of the Society with less restraint than they would naturally feel

in a mixed congregation. In the higher departments
of ministry they are alike to be under a covering of
the Spirit that will give authority to each utterance.
Of late men and women hold their meetings for discipline together, in some places, the nature of their
business and the growing freedom of intercourse ren-
dering this method, in some cases, practicable.

From what has been said it is obvious that to place
a woman over a congregation of men and women as
an official pastor, or minister-in-chief, is an unnatural
proceeding, to be justified only by the law of necessity. It may be thus defended in exceptional cases,
where the right man is wanting, or the phenominal
woman present. Woman is unsexed by such a position, and therefore the practice can never become
common. This fact renders the exercise of woman's
gifts in the ministry difficult and embarrassing as
churches are commonly organized. In many places
she is now encouraged to use her freedom in the
more private meetings of the church, and not unfrequently, when her ability has been proved, she is in-
vited to speak from the pulpit. But this is by cour-
tesy, not of right; and the limited opportunities thus
offered are not sufficient to develop her gifts and cultivate her talents for any extended usefulness as a
preacher.

The radical changes introduced by the Quakers
gave woman an opportunity to prove the God-given
endowment not lacking in her, when an even chance

is afforded. Nobly has she attested her right, as a sister, to plead for the salvation of perishing souls, and to comfort, as men seldom know how, the afflicted. In almost equal numbers with men, the faithful mothers in Israel have labored and suffered, have borne and triumphed, under the cross and banner of Him, whose advent and resurrection holy women were foremost to announce. This is one of the most valuable achievements of that band of radical reformers, who were not content with merely cutting off a few growths of error, but went straight to the root of all the perversions in the Church, and laid again the foundation of Christian liberty in brotherly equality before God. It is not impossible that the highest benefit the world and the Church will gain from the advent of Quakerism is to be found in the proofs and illustrations it affords of various important truths. Several of these truths have already been recognized by the public, and others are obtaining more general acknowledgement; so that if the Society should perish it would not have lived in vain, having merged much of its spirit into more prosperous organizations.

The completeness of the reformation effected by Friends in their own society, in restoring the primitive simplicity and freedom of Christian worship, made it easy for women to do their part in the religious service without conflicting with any class privileges. How the impediment of a stated ministry,

with a service uncontrolled by the immediate promptings of the Spirit, is to be overcome doth not yet appear. Perhaps the initial steps are already being
taken in the education of a new class of female
preachers of almost every denomination in our
Women's Christian Temperance Unions. The Gospel is often as well and forcibly taught, and its spirit
vitally diffused, in the work of these organizations, as
in any avowed church service. Nor do men feel
themselves at all dishonored in listening to these
modern Deborahs and Judiths and Phebes and Pris-
cillas, while they proclaim the gospel of Temperance,
and boldly show their brothers their duty in regard
to it. Ministers drop into these Gospel Meetings of
the united sisterhood, and sit as respectful listeners
while women pray, and exhort each other to more
zeal and courage, and read or extemporize addresses,
which have all the qualities of the Sabbath sermon,
with a little more practical application to the immediate business of resisting the tide of sin which is
bearing down brothers and sons and fathers to common ruin, under the sanction of law. These men,
thus listening while their sisters take up the work
which they themselves too often neglect, are not de-
graded by their polite attention, but go out some
inches taller than they came in. And so it will be
when woman is allowed her proper share in the ordinary services of the Church. There is not a place on
earth where men are more manly than they are in a

good Quaker meeting, where brothers and sisters, fathers and mothers, in mutual respect and love, unite their hearts and voices in praising God and inspiring each other with greater earnestness in His service.

The truth is, extremely few ministers preach a whole gospel. Nor could they do so were they to try ever so faithfully. Only one in a thousand is constituted after the pattern of Him in whom male and female so perfectly blended that from the loftiest heights of doctrine He could turn with a mother's tenderness and heal the wounded heart, or win a timid child to His arms. Few, like the grand and loving Apostle Paul, can be "all things to all men"—chasten like a father and weep like a mother over her erring sons. Ordinary people are like the fragments of a broken bowl, capable of holding but a few spoonfuls of water or milk. It is only when we are united in a proper manner that we can carry enough of the gospel of God's grace to supply the needs of thirsty souls. This is why religious services are usually so unattractive to the masses. Make them what they should be, give them the proper spirit and variety, and our churches would soon be filled with interested and eager listeners. This is proved by the fact that a many-sided man who can pour out both wisdom and love in ample measure is never in want of an audience. Some are great in sections and attract for a time, but finally weary their listeners with one kind of discourse.

The remedy for all this is to be found in a proper development and combination of the manifold gifts of the Spirit in every church where men and women meet to worship God, to edify one another, and to instruct and persuade people of all minds to give themselves to Christ. That woman's voice, (when she does not assume the role of theological professor) is potent for this congenial office, thousands can bear witness. Men are not less open than women to this maternal ministry, when it is of the right kind. Perhaps they are even more open, for the lines of moral influence often strengthen as they cross the sexual margin.

Precisely in what way women will become reinstated in all their natural, and therefore Divine, rights cannot be foreseen ; but the result is as certain as the law of progress. It is a hopeful sign of the times when a leading minister in one of the most conservative denominations, (Theodore L. Cuyler, D. D.) can publish such language as the following in a popular religious newspaper, and pass unchallenged. He first fortifies himself with a good endorser by saying, "An eminent Episcopal Clergyman once said to me, 'Elizabeth Fry had as clear a call from God to preach as I have, or any Bishop in the land.'" Then, after speaking of the modest Quakeress's first trials, he adds:

"Elizabeth Fry soon became an acknowledged minister,' and addressed great multitudes of people in Great Britain and on the Continent for thirty-five years. The Holy Spirit owned her instructive and Scriptural discourses to the conversion and edification of many souls. Her case is a sufficient answer to the absurd dogma that God never calls a woman to proclaim His glorious Gospel. Would that there were a thousand like her to-day to confront the rampant skepticism and worldliness of the time!"

X.

PEACE.

The Quakers have always been open and consistent advocates of Peace. Peace at any price has been their doctrine, since nothing appears to them more directly opposed to the spirit of Christianity than war. Even defensive warfare they hold to be forbidden by the precepts of Christ. "Love your enemies; bless them that curse you ; do good to them that hate you." "If any man smite thee on one cheek turn to him the other also." "If thine enemy hunger feed him, if he thirst give him drink," etc. War is the reverse of all this. Havoc and destruction lie evermore in its path, and soul-sickness and moral degeneracy attend its footsteps. Can a Christian be thus engaged?

It is perhaps too much to say that this is not possible: and yet it might be affirmed with truth, that a *perfect* Christian will seldom or never be found thus employed. Can we imagine Paul and John, in the maturity of their abounding love for men, leading their fellows to battle? "Why not them," you may ask, "as well as David and Joshua?" Because they are under another dispensation, and have drank at

the new fountain opened in Calvary. Christ came to
lay down His life for others, and not to take the lives
of others. It was this new, Divine way of overcom-
ing evil by love and patient endurance of wrong that
created the distinctive glory of the Christian dispensation. Jesus could have resisted those who arrested
Him, with perfect ease. It was to prove this, that,
by a bold confession of Himself and a masterful power accompanying His words, He caused the whole
company of His pursuers to fall back prostrate. For
the same reason He allowed two of His disciples to
carry swords and then forbade them to use them.
Power was not wanting; twelve legions of angels
waited his whispered prayer: but the world could
not be saved by power. Men cannot be compelled to
love God by force of arms. That is the Mohamme-
dan theory, which God suffered to be illustrated
when Christendom so far apostatized from her Lord's
example as to resort to carnal weapons. Jesus very
well understood, that the Jews must have His blood
before the power of sin could be broken by the transfer of the pure life of God, thus revealed to them,
into their convicted souls. Only from this heavenly
fountain would life eternal spring again in the arid
desert of human depravity. What had before been
done was a preparation for this final act of salvation.
This is the mystery of the Cross. By this the em-
pire of Satan, which had resisted all other appliances,
received its mortal wound. The Law was a sword to

cleave the national heart and conscience, that the
waiting Branch of heavenly Glory might be engrafted
on the bleeding stock of Judaism.

All this necessitates a similar spirit in the ministers and followers of the *Lamb of God*, who alone can
take away the sins of the world. This is the law of
discipleship ; and men are required to obey it as far
as they are able. This is the perfect standard for
Christian men and Christian nations. But unfortunately there are few of the former and none of the
latter. The leaven which was long ago "hid in three
measures of meal" is slowly working out its results,
and the end will be peace—peace to the heart, and
peace to the nation which lays aside its carnal weapons and uses only the arms of truth and reason, being
clothed in the armor of love. Suffering may indeed
come, perhaps death, but to such as find it possible to
follow Him who through death destroyed that which
brought death into the world, a more glorious life is
assured. To those who do not find this course possible it remains to approach it as nearly as they are
able.

The great majority of Christians are still passing
through the Mosaic dispensation ; for every man has
to taste of all the experiences of that "peculiar people," elected of God through the faith of Abraham to
illustrate on a grand scale the law and method of human salvation. It is a long distance upward from the
first act of renouncing one's own native country (the

world) at the call of God, to the dissolution of all
earthly ties, and going forth, as a spirit raised from
the dead, to seek and save a lost world, as did Spiritual Israel on the demise of the national body.
Hence many promising disciples of Christ long exhibit the qualities of Joshua, David and Peter, whose
virtues were genuine and of a high order; but not
the highest. To such as these war in a just cause is
no more unlawful than it was to those worthies, until
they receive the command, "Put up thy sword into
his sheath". Then they are to advance and leave to
others that part of virtue's defences.

Friends have never denied this qualifying principle,
but have claimed the right to follow their highest
convictions and leave others to do likewise, always
upholding the highest Christian standard for individuals and for nations. When not permitted to enjoy
the rights of conscience peaceably they have submit-
ted to whatever exactions were made upon them, so
far as they felt at liberty. In one particular I think
their scruples exceeded the demand of sound reason.
They refused to pay taxes levied to support war, preferring to let their property be taken. But property
is the creature of Government; and to surrender, on
peremptory demand, a portion of that which Government has enabled us to acquire is not sanctioning the
acts of that Government, but a common duty, as
Christ showed when he gave tribute to Cæsar of that
which was Cæsar's. On this point the Quakers went

to an extreme and became resistants in the cause of non-resistance. To yield to a demand for money, or to pay a Government tax, is not a contribution, and does not differ essentially from allowing proderty to be taken away. The same is true of paying tithes. While the law required it Friends might have paid the tax, and carried on their moral warfare against the obnoxious laws until they were repealed. By so doing they would have saved themselves much suffering, since this form of resistance was the cause of many of their persecutions; but their course may have called attention more forcibly to the wrongs thus conspicuously reproved.

It may be alleged that our personal service in war is also due to the State in return for common defence; but this trenches on personal liberty when such defence is not asked for. The distinction is well indicated by the author of Marmion :—

> "My manors, halls and bowers shall still
> Be open at my Sovereign's will—
> My castles are my King's alone,
> From turret to foundation stone—
> The *hand* of Douglass is his own."

But there is another important qualification to the principle of non-resistance. All its virtue lies in the end sought. Submission to wrong through mere weakness or tenderness of feeling has no merit. The object of Christ was to do good, to gain a moral victory; and where this is not possible the obligation

ceases. Jesus would not have surrendered his life
to a band of highwaymen. He gave it to the Jewish
nation and the world, for an object worthy the
sacrifice.

A Christian has no right to throw away his life,
with all its possibilities of good, if attacked by brutes
in human form. To do so is casting pearls before
swine. Christ did not abrogate the natural law of self-
defense, but supplemented it with a higher law of
saving love, making it our duty to save the life of the
soul, and even the souls of our enemies, when possible, by the sacrifice of what has less value. But
when this end is not attainable, the law of nature remains in force. Of this God and the imperilled man
must judge.

And if a man have not the spirit of a martyr he is
not to be condemned, as before stated, for wanting
what is not yet given him. We must reach as high
as we can, and let others reach beyond us. "There is
one glory of the sun, and another glory of the moon,
and another glory of the stars, for one star differeth
from another star in glory." So there is a patriotism
which is truly glorious and yet falls below the glory
of the Cross, as far as the majesty of night is excelled
by the splendors of day. All this may be admitted
in favor of a just defence, and of war waged in a
righteous cause.

The case entirely differs where the war is aggressive, or where the injury resisted is slight. To sup-

port national pride or selfishness in the pursuit of aggrandizement or unchristian revenge is no man's duty; and were all Christians faithful in this respect to refuse compliance with the unjust requirements of their rulers, war in civilized countries would soon cease. The extremely low standard of duty among professing Christians in this great matter is worthy of all reprehension, and the disgrace and injury suffered by the Church in consequence cannot be measured. The conduct of nominal Christian nations in trampling on all the laws of justice, to say nothing of charity, often without a word of protest from the Church, is one of the greatest hindrances to the spread of Christianity among those we call heathen. Almost alone among the daughters of Zion the little band of those who trembled at his word has stood faithfully by the Prince of Peace, and struggled to uphold his fallen banner. Shall it be in vain?

Already the skies are brightening; though, alas! it is not the united Church that is calling with powerful voice for the sword to return to its sheath. Individual statesmen and philanthropists, in sufficient numbers to be heard, are at length joining in the plea for peace, and the worthy example of two great nations has given hopeful impetus to the cause of Arbitration.

Great reforms come in the air and spread from Heaven downward, like a clearing sky. The finger of God sends an electric current through the world and

presently the poet's dream and the prophet's promise
are realized. So may the rainbow of Peace blossom
speedily on the long and dreary deluge of human
bloodshed.

And when the storms of battle have passed away
and the sunshine of God's love rests, with healing
power, on a brotherhood of happy nations, men will
assuredly recall with grateful approval the protest
of the gentle-souled Quakers against the sad anomaly
of "Christian warfare."

XI.

On the question Temperance the Friends, as a body, have held the advance of all other religious societies. Not that religious people are not generally temperate, so far as their religion is genuine, but as bodies, speaking unitedly, and with authority to their members, and to the world, in the name of the Master, the churches have not fulfilled their duty in this great matter, which, next to Peace, and perhaps even before it, is the most important work of public reform still demanding their attention. Owing to their greater numbers, and larger admixture of worldly elements, more popular branches of the Church have too often ignored their high obligation to speak with ememphasis and authority on both of these great questions.

From the days of its founder Quakerism has had a voice that could be heard and understood by all who would listen. Several times a year, at regular intervals, the following, among other searching "queries," is read to all the members, and an answer required to be sent up to the more general Meetings for Discipline—"Are Friends careful to avoid the unnecessary use of spiritous liquors, and all other beverages of an intoxicating character, and frequenting places where they are sold; and do they avoid attending places of amusement of a hurtful tendency?" Suitable advices accompany the inquiry, and if delinquents are found incorrigible they are subject to disownment, after faithful brotherly efforts for their recovery.

In addition, the Book of Discipline, to be found in every well-furnished family, contains the following admonitions:

"In consideration of the corrupting and ruinous effects occasioned by the importation, distillation, fermentation, and sale of alcoholic spirits, which produce intemperance, and lead to the impoverishment of many, the injury of the constitution and minds of many more, and the increase of vice and dissolution in the land; it is earnestly desired that none of our members contribute to this great evil by being concerned in importing, distilling, selling alcoholic or fermented liquors, or using them, except for purposes strictly medicinal, or selling their grain or other produce for the purpose of distillation or fermentation.

"If any shall so far disregard the concern of the Society and the labor of their friends, as to continue in any of these practices, or give way to habits of intemperance from any cause whatever, and cannot be brought to such a sense of their misconduct as to desist from it, they should receive the care of the Overseers.

"As wine, cider, and other fermented liquors possess intoxicating qualities, their use has more or less tendency to the same evils as the stronger liquors. Friends should therefore avoid and discourage their use, manufacture, or sale.

"We would affectionately advise and entreat all our members to be careful in the use of intoxicating liquors, even for medicinal purposes, lest the appetite grow upon them and they be ruined thereby, or, should they themselves escape, lest their example lead to the ruin of others.

"Friends are advised to abstain from the use of Tobacco. It is deleterious in its effects, often laying the foundation of serious diseases. It is an expensive habit, generally offensive to those not accustomed to it, and frequently leads to other evil practices."

As with regard to slavery and some other customs of long standing, Friends did not come all at once to the full recognition of what the highest duty would finally require. Many continued the moderate use of what were the common articles of drink and were generally supposed to be more or less necessary and beneficial, if used with proper caution, until advancing science has at length shown the mistake. As fast as new light dawned they moved with it, farther and farther from the path of danger and temptation, hop-

ing to save all who could be influenced from the way
that leads so stealthily, but often so surely, to ruin.

With such a record they are prepared to enter
earnestly into any general movement which the Spirit of Reform may inaugurate for the deliverance of
the whole or any part of the race from this worse
than African bondage. Those now to be delivered,
or protected against the worst form of slavery, are
not strangers to us, but the flower and strength of our
homes, our fathers, brothers, sons ; and we might also
add, our mothers, sisters and daughters. Of course
we ourselves are never in danger ! And from what do
they, our heart's companions, our country's hope, the
makers of the present and future of this great world,
ask to be protected by the State? Must it be answered, in this nineteenth century of Christianity,
From the open, legalized, persuasive tender, to young
and old, of the poison cup, whose first tasting is so
often the first step in the road to earthly, and perhaps eternal perdition?

Has Manhood, with all its wealth of divine endowment, all its masterly achievements over the forces of
Nature, risen as yet no higher than this level? What
will the great open-eyed Future say of us—those who
are to be our judges, because they are the heirs of all
the misery we leave to them by our action, or our in-
action? Will they not regard us much as we regard
our sleepy-souled ancestors who got up from their
drunken revels, their gaming tables, their fist and

dagger fights, their "glorious victories" in war or commercial plunder, and went into the "Sanctuary" to give thanks for the mercies they had received?

And what is the Church doing, all this while?— that Militant Church " bright as the sun, clear as the moon, and terrible as an army with banners," the dread of all forms of iniquity and licentiousness? Is she calling, with united voice, on the trafficers in human woe to desist from their naughty devices, and cease to deal out moral disease and death in the community? Is she calling on legislators, with a unanimity of purpose demanding respect, to put innocence, rather than vice, under the shield of law ; and warning the ministers of the law that both interest and duty require their attention to the claims of humanity? Were such her voice and attitude on this great question, can any one doubt the result?

As to the most practicable means of restricting and finally abolishing the liquor traffic, Friends, like other thoughtful people, are not wholly agreed. Their general temper inclines them to mild and pacific methods, and non-political action ; but some agree with the more radical wing of the gathering armies of Freedom, that the time has arrived for decisive action, as come it must, sooner or later. They believe that the vast moneyed interests involved in the iniquitous traffic with wakeful and unprincipled men to guard them, will succeed in holding the rival political parties inactive, until their grip is broken by a flank movement of the party of reform. They remember how the defiant Slave Oligarchy was overthrown, and see a striking resemblance in the present contest. When a great and organized evil is being pressed to the wall it is sure to give battle before surrendering; and the stress of its position, calling forth more and more violent efforts for defence, often precipitates the final conflict at a time when least expected. Much the same difference of opinion exists now among Temperance reformers as existed among the opponents of Slavery before the Rebellion. Perhaps neither opinion is adequate for the case, but if the time for deliverance has come the jarring of thunder will condense the clouds into rain, and the convergent winds will pack them together and hurry on the storm.

Moral Suasion must not abate its efforts; but neither should it suppose the mild west wind alone is going to bring rain enough to wash away this burning curse that has held the race in bondage since Noah's day. Avarice that can sow death and degradation broadcast without a qualm of conscience is made of sterner stuff than that. He who could quicken the dead to life with His marvelous touch and word, found many devils that had to be commanded before they would leave their victims. When Bacchus and Mammon combine their Legions, Love and Authority will both have to speak before they will quit their respectable lodgings and go into the herd of swine where they belong.

A good illustration of the course which sometimes proves most effective is given in the story of two sisters, in ———, whose husbands had purchased a hotel and were carrying on the "honorable" trade, with some disgust of their own, and more of their Christian wives, who often remonstrated, but were met with the ready argument that there was no other way to succeed, and pay their debt for the property. The sisters prayed and suffered till they could bear it no longer, feeling ashamed to walk the streets. At length they resolved on their course, and sent a request for their husbands to meet them in the parlor. When arrived, the ladies informed their attentive partners that the limit of endurance was reached, and they could have their choice, to remove the liquor from the house, or let them go back that night to their father's. Being men of sense, the husbands replied goodnaturedly, "Why this means *business*, does n't it?" and handing the fair victors the keys, told them to go and do as they liked. They went, and had a good time breaking every bottle and emptying every cask of liquor in the house. Then they set about making the hotel doubly attractive to guests, with pleasant ornaments and solid comforts, and in a few years the debt was paid, and a happy home remained, a real resting-place for the weary, and often heart-hungry traveler.

Perhaps if the Christian Church and the Party of Reform were to say unitedly to the two great parties that undertake the political management of the nation, " We can bear this prostration and shame no longer : take away the ' accursed thing' which causes us to bury our faces in the dust before our enemies, or we will forsake you, much as we have loved you in the past, and put our trust in a Father who will not fail us," the far-seeing statesmen, who really wish them success, but dare not trust the Right, might also understand that it " means business," and agree to give them the key of the situation by putting the law, and power for its enforcement wholly on the side of common morality, national thrift, clean lives, and happy homes.

XII.

True culture unites with religion in recommending simplicity of life and manners. The person of refined taste prefers the simplest and most natural style of expression, and what language is to thought, clothing is to the person. Beyond mere utility, language and dress are to some extent an index of the mental condition. Perhaps it would be too much to say that they also betoken the moral condition, though unmistakably, it is sometimes true. Great allowance must be made for circumstances, but where there is full liberty of choice, dress and style of utterance pretty accurately bespeak the man. Sometimes dress bespeaks both the man and the age. It is not long since "gentlemen" ruffled and bedecked themselves like our present women of fashion. Grave judges, bishops and statesmen looked like children dressed for a masquerade. Race-growth and enlightenment have wrought a healthful change in this respect for the male sex, and the same law is working slowly for the emancipation of woman, but at a disadvantage, because personal appearance has more to do with a woman's fortune than with a man's.

Friends met the exactions of fashion with a strong and decisive rebuke. They refused to change their external appearance at the bidding of court or clown. In carrying out their principles they may have done some violence to the natural love of beauty and variety, but there were important gains in return. Temptation lost much of its power to the plainly attired young men and women who bore the cross and despised the shame, while the pecuniary saving to those who dressed plainly often made the difference between riches and poverty. The worse than waste of costly changes in dress not unfrequently holds families which might rise to competency, in perpetual. bondage to care and toil. It also ties up the hands of charity; and, perhaps, checks even the impulse to give, by the constant devotion of every energy to selfish ends. Another motive to simplicity is the setting of a good example. Even where there is ability to dress extravagantly, brotherly love will think of one's neighbors, and have no wish to outshine them, or tempt them to go beyond their means. Very laudable has been the spirit shown by Friends in general in this matter, and one consequence has been a very small percentage of poverty in the Society. And their poor have always been kindly cared for and treated as equals.

The rigors of discipline are now greatly relaxed in many portions of the Society in regard to dress, as well as in other particulars, though the principle of plainness is still strongly recommended. The distinctive marks are passing away, as they should do to a reasonable extent; for adherence to a certain style for all is not natural, and taste may fairly be exercised to a limited extent in adapting dress to those peculiarities of person by which nature distinguishes us one from another, and also in gratifying a healthful love of variety. Sameness is found in no part of God's creation. Even "one star differeth from another in glory." Everything proves that God loves variety as well as order and beauty.

No doubt the Friends erred in adhering too long to the style of dress which was in vogue among serious people at the time of their origin; and especially in insisting upon it in the case of their children. Besides this, to make any non-essential a test of piety and social standing, is extremely dangerous. It leads directly toward formalism, and is apt to end in Pharisaism on the one hand and dislike of religion on the other.

In the matter of "plain language" Friends undertook a controversy which had moral significance at the time, but lost it when the innovations complained of had established themselves as a part of the national speech. As Dr. Trench correctly observes "words are not necessarily rooted in their etymology." They are merely instruments for conveying ideas, and change their import according to the use generally made of them. Sunday is not now the sun's day, nor

Thursday Thor's day, and these names are as harmless as meat which has been sacrificed to idols, unless we have a "conscience of the idol," for "the earth is the Lord's and the fullness thereof." Suppose a coin issued to carry on unjust war ·falls into your hands long after the war has ceased, must you decline to use it? Has the metal become corrupt? Words are merely the coin of our mental exchanges, vehicles of our ideas; and retain no character of their own.

A tender conscience is most commendable and lovely; but God can scarcely wish to see His children suffer inconvenience and pain for a mistaken idea. It is, therefore, to be regretted that Friends have retained these peculiarities of speech so long. They not only embarrass their intercourse with other people and deter some who might like to associate with them, but they lessen popular confidence in the practical good sense of the Society.

There is no more impropriety in using the personal pronoun *you* in addressing one or more persons, than in using the relative *who* in like manner. Although it was foolish and unchristian flattery which first dictated the use of the plural pronoun in addressing individuals of rank, the shorter and more easily spoken word finally supplanted its slow and stately competitor, and established itself as a part of the national dialect. This ended the controversy in its moral aspects. When master and servant received the same address the spirit of flattery which once defiled

the word "you" took its departure to return no more
and conscience was, or should have been released.
But the Friends could not occupy their liberty. Had
not their fathers been called by the Spirit of Truth to
take up this cross and carry it through much persecution? And should their children now lay it down?
They could not find the heart to do so; and hence
they have continued to bear it with more or less faithfulness to the present time. Few, however, excepting
those born and reared in the Society, find any obligation to assume the distinctive badge, and so pass by
the little wicket gate which leads into the quiet fields
of Quakerism where a few humble souls meet apart
to worship the God of their fathers in the silence of
all flesh, under the shadow of an ancient cross.

Very pleasant it is to hear the friendly "thee" and
"thou," and look upon the neat and simple costume
of these honored disciples of Him who wore a seamless
coat. But their imitation is not so literal as to in-
duce them to wear seamless tunics, or speak the language of the first Christians. It was most clearly a
departure from their general principle to follow the
letter rather than the spirit, in these external matters,
and thus make the "narrow way" still narrower with
needless burdens. There are quite enough necessary
crosses to try the hearts and develop the strength of
all who will make truth and simplicity the rules of
their lives. In hedging their lot in the great Fold
with these artificial barriers, Friends not o y becam

formalists while decrying the formality of others
but they also hedged out the fresh life which
should have come to them from the world which
it is their most important business to convert.

XIII.

DISUSE OF TYPICAL RITES.

" The apostle shows the Christian religion to be in truth and substance what the Jewish was only in type and shadow."—Archbishop Tillotson.

"Are ye so foolish? having begun in the Spirit are ye now made perfect by the flesh?" "Know ye therefore that they which are of faith the same are the children of Abraham. And the scripture, foreseeing that God would justify the heathen by faith, preached before the gospel unto Abraham, saying, In thee shall all nations be blessed." . . " Wherefore the law was our schoolmaster to bring us unto Christ, that we might be justified by faith. But after that faith is come we are no longer under a schoolmaster. For ye are all the children of God by faith in Christ Jesus, For as many of you as have been baptized into Christ have put on Christ. There is neither Jew nor Greek, there is neither bond nor free, there is neither male nor female ; for ye are all one in Christ Jesus. And if ye be Christ's then are ye Abraham's seed, and heirs according to the promise." "Stand fast therefore in the liberty wherewith Christ has

made us free, and be not entangled again in the yoke
of bondage." . . . "For we through the Spirit
wait for the hope of righteousness by faith. For in
Jesus Christ neither circumcision availeth anything
nor uncircumcision, but faith which worketh by
love."—Paul to the Galatians.

All this the Friends applied, not only to the law of
Moses and the forms that grew up under it, but also
to what they regarded as the stepping stones left by
Christ to lead Jewish converts gradually up to the
higher level of a pure spiritual religion in which faith
works by love to the purification of heart and life.
This was the end of all those external acts whose
special object was to illustrate certain profound truths
of the human soul and its relations, much as a schoolmaster draws a diagram on the blackboard to assist
the pupil to a comprehension of laws too subtle for
his present mental grasp. But after the truth has
gained its place in the mind and transformed the diagram into a mental image capable of being recalled
at any moment, the figure on the blackboard is of no
further use, and may even occupy the attention so as
to hinder progress.

Water-baptism and the eucharist are symbolical representations of those acts whereby the soul is cleansed
through divine grace, and fed with the truth and love
of God, as embodied in Christ Jesus, the "bread
which came down from heaven" and was broken for
sinful men. And only so far as these outward sym-

bols can aid us in the mental and moral apprehension
of Christ are they of any special use. If the mind
rests in the figure and does not look through it to the
thing signified the type becomes a veil to the mental
eve instead of a magnifier, as was intended. And
whensoever the substance can be as fully apprehended without its use, the figure ceases to be of value
and is "ready to pass away." Its further employment may be as inappropriate as it would be to sit
down in a friend's presence and read letters which
he had sent in his absence, to keep us in remembrance
of him.

"As often as ye eat this bread and drink this cup ye
do show forth the Lord's death *till he come*," said Paul
to the Corinthians, referring to Christ's words, "This
do, as oft as ye drink it, in remembrance of me." The
rite is thus limited, in express terms, to the period of
the Lord's absence from his Church: and so it is regarded by all. The question of continuing the me-
morial service turns then on the Lord's absence and
what that includes. If he meant, as is generally supposed by Christians, during his absence in visible bodily form, then the continuance is justified. But if he
meant until he should return in the power of the
Spirit to establish that kingdom which "cometh without observation," in the hearts and minds of his disciples, or among the nations of the earth, then the
time may be past, or passing; or past to some, and
passing to others: or optional to the believer, as

something he may choose or decline without offence to love.

Jesus said plainly to his disciples, "I will not leave you comfortless, I will come to you. Yet a little while, and the world seeth me no more, but ye see me." "If any man love me he will keep my words, and my Father will love him, and we will come to him and make our abode with him."

It is this potential return, this abiding presence of the Father and Son, in the communion of spirit with Spirit, that Friends regard as containing the fulfillment of Christ's blessed promises. Already the world is judged in us and by us. Already the living and dead are standing before the great white throne of God's righteousness. The sheep are constantly passing to the right and the goats to the left as fast as one enters the gates of life eternal and another the broad way that leads to destruction. With a death-rate of one every second of time on this small planet, can the hosts of gathered ages be more easily judged at some future day of reckoning than now, as they pass along the great highway of human life, and each, by a final decision of his own free will, takes the right hand or the left, while the Word of God stands as a radiant guide-board to point the way of life and the way of death? "He that rejecteth me, and receiveth not my words, hath one that judgeth him: the word that I have spoken, the same shall judge him in the last day."

But whatever may be anticipated as to a final judgment, it is certain that Christ did return and embrace all his disciples, baptizing them individually and collectively with the Holy Spirit, in so marked a manner that his prayer was fully answered—" as, thou, Father, art in me and I in thee, that they also may be one in us." It is equally certain that he came in judgment to the Jewish nation, as he expressly declared he would do, while some who heard his great prophecy were still living. By these acts the old earth and old heavens were removed, consumed with fire, and a new earth and new heavens created, wherein dwelt, not " a shadow of good things to come " but the things themselves—faith, hope, charity, truth, joy, peace, all the fruits of the Spirit, the righteousness of the saints.

In these important facts there is ample justification for any Christian who may feel released from a part or the whole of the typical system of religious instruction. However useful that system may have been in an earlier day, or may still be to some, the genius of Christianity, which does not hold in check, but fully coincides with the law of progress seen in all God's works, distinctly points to a time when all external types and symbols will have rendered up their contents and passed from sight. They are easily and naturally transformed into *language* which serves as a kind of resurrection body for the knowledge to which they gave birth; and when this has been accomplished there should be no going back to "the weak and beggarly elements" of an earlier dispensation. As well might the emancipated spirit come back and gather up, not the handful of dust only which it leaves for the grave, but all that has ever aided its development, and which, when used, it has scattered on every wind and stream and place of earth where it has walked, taking all these again to its embrace, instead of the spiritualized results of their action. It is perhaps only consistent that those who anticipate such an experience for the body should try to immortalize at least a portion of the forms in which religion once walked upon the earth.

But why should those who think two of those ancient forms binding on the Church, object if others consider seven of equal obligation? or if still others would revive the whole Jewish ritual, since Christ observed every tittle of the law, and many of his disciples, even after the day of Pentacost, were scrupulous about the practices in which they had been educated? Where shall we draw the line? If any man will divest his mind of the effects of his education and look at the question fairly I believe he will acknowledge that there is no stopping place short of perfect liberty to discontinue any and all of these helps to knowledge when their aid is no longer needed. This is what the Friends have done. Knowing what baptism means by their knowledge of the action of water on the body, they apply to the Foun-

tain of "living waters" to have their souls cleansed of
sin's defilements.   The love of God is all that can effect such a result.   This brings forth the Godly sorrow which worketh repentance not to be repented of.
And what water will not remove the same divine energy consumes by a baptism of fire, acting with more
intense and searching enmity toward all that is offensive to God and injurious to the soul.   This is suc-
ceeded by the endowment of the Spirit—or rather,
that which thoroughly cleanses also endows the soul
with spiritual power to walk in the life, and work the
works of God.   Whoever experiences this baptism of
the Spirit is made one with Christ and thenceforth
feeds upon His life, as the branch feeds upon the vine,
or as our bodies feed upon the fruits of the earth,
which are represented by the bread and wine—wine
being a striking symbol of the love of Christ expressed
to us in His sufferings and death.   But water is also
a fit symbol of that love by which all our inward life
is nourished and kept active ; and whoever wishes and
has eyes to see, can behold the mysteries of redemption illustrated, not once a month or once in three
months, but every day, as he partakes of the bread
broken for his body's sustenance, or eats the flesh
of the lamb or bullock sacrificed for his needs, or
drinks the water drawn from the pierced bosom of the
earth, or the fresh juice of crushed fruits.   "This do *as
oft as ye drink it* in remembrance of me."   This is the
final attainment of perfected love and knowledge, to

recognize the Lord in all the acts of life, so that we can say with Paul, "I live, yet not I but Christ liveth in me." " For me to live is Christ and to die is gain." We shall then understand what he meant when he said to the Corinthians, " I speak to wise men ; judge ye what I say. The cup of blessing which we bless, is it not the communion of the blood of Christ? The bread which we break, is it not the communion of the body of Christ? For we being many are one bread and one body ; for we are all partakers of that one Bread."

It is this daily communion that Friends desire, and they fear that attaching a mystical importance to an occasional act of fellowship tends to satisfy the conscience and divert the mind from that constant feeding on the Heavenly Loaf which our spiritual health demands.

So also with regard to baptism ; one who has been baptized with water, according to the rule of the Church, is apt to feel that he has complied with the Lord's will and is now a member of the covenant household of grace, while his heart may be as far as ever from that holiness without which no man shall see God. Nor does the baptism of the Spirit, which Christ came specially to administer, seem to be looked for as an essential consequence of the acceptance of the gospel. Thus the Church moves along a low plane of experience requiring little that men of the world cannot comply with, and doing little to elevate thought above the semblances of divine things.

As to any specific commands bearing upon these outward symbols it is easy to see that they have a double reference, like many of Christ's utterances; and the fact that he neither baptized with water himself, nor partook of the emblematic supper, saying to his disciples, "I will not eat it until it be fulfilled in the kingdom of God," indicates that these figures were not of those fundamental things that should not pass away, but belonged to the transition period, when the Church was passing through the penumbra of the Jewish dispensation to the full freedom and light of the Gospel. "My words are spirit and they are life;" this gives the key to all Christ's deeper sayings. His last commission to his followers, "Go, make disciples of all nations, baptizing them into the name of the Father, and of the Son, and of the Holy Ghost," may with perfect consistency be understood of a spiritual baptism, since he had a little before said to them, "As my Father hath sent me, even so send I you;" and then breathing on them, added, "Receive ye the Holy Ghost: whosoever sins ye remit they are remitted unto them, and whosoever sins ye retain they are retained." John xx, 21-23. These words import a full transfer of his official functions to his representatives while they abide in him, and the event proved the gift to be not in word only, but in substance, for three thousand souls were converted on the first great outpouring of the Spirit of God through those who had just received the endowment of power from on high.

These things, taken in connection with the fact that Jesus did not himself baptize with water, and the declaration of Paul, " Christ sent me not to baptize (with water) but to preach the gospel, (I Cor., i, 17,) amount to a demonstration that the celebrated commission did not enjoin the continuance of a rite which belonged specifically to the Jewish and transition periods.

If it be asked why the apostles continued to use water baptism the answer is, for the same reason that they continued to circumcise and do many other things they were accustomed to which formed no part of the gospel dispensation, but were permitted for a time, until faith could walk without external helps. Till that time comes it is not unlawful to use symbols, and the fact that they are so tenaciously held by the Church in this late day indicates, though it does not prove, that they have some present utility.   All that any should ask is liberty to follow his best judgment without dictation, or undue constraint upon conscience.   The question will then reach an easy and natural solution, and no wrong be done to any.   But while the great body of the Christian Churches makes the acceptance of any outward sign a condition of fellowship, and while these signs are, as they have ever been since the Church turned back into the wilderness and refused her birthright of liberty, a root of discord among brethren, it is needful that there should be some to prove that the grace of God requires no such

auxiliaries where the light of Christ is permitted to
shine with ray direct upon the soul. "For the kingdom of God is not eating and drinking, but righteousness and peace and joy in the Holy Ghost."

That multitudes have found peace and comfort in
compliance with what they believed to be their duty
in these respects is undeniable; but so equally does
the pious Catholic in his faithful attendance at Mass,
and his Friday fasting; so does the pious Quaker in
submitting to say "thou" instead of "you," and to
wear a certain style of dress; and so does the pious
Hindoo in satisfying his conscience by afflicting his
body. And so long as neither can do better it is perhaps no kindness to deprive them of these modes of
exercising their moral faculties and deriving that
healthful glow of conscience on which our happiness
so much depends. Herein God has shown his
greatness in leaving us the free use of these various
means of grace—for grace can only reach through the
exercise of our moral faculties—until higher and better means are made available. But when any of these
means come to be regarded as essential, and made objects of superstitious veneration, the healthful effect
is vitiated, and a ferment of decay engendered
which produces the flatulence of spiritual vanity and
pride. It is then better that they should be removed,
or at least that we should understand our case, and
learn to attribute effects to their real causes.

What Quakerism teaches and insists upon is that

DISUSE OF TYPICAL RITES

men shall not substitute a shadow for the substance
on which their eternal welfare depends—that they
be baptized in reality, with water from, (or as our
Baptist brethren prefer to have it, *in*) that river
which proceeds from the throne of God, and which,
while it nourishes virtue, destroys both sin and its
effects; and that beyond this the innermost seeds
of evil, the covetousness from which all sin flows,
shall be consumed in the renovating fire of Christ's
love, whereby all things are made new, and man
again united to God in the fellowship and power
of the Spirit: That in this new life they shall
feed upon Christ as our bodies feed on the fruits of
Nature, or as the branch feeds upon the vine, His
words and spirit conveying the truth and love of
God to the dependent soul, in that communion of
thought and feeling which constitutes the joy and
glory of the heavenly state. "This is life eternal, to
know Thee, the only true God and Jesus Christ whom
Thou hast sent:" That whoever is a participant of
these divine verities has no need of signs whose
office is to foreshadow an approaching reality, they
having realized the truth of Christ's language, "My
words are spirit and they are life." "I am the living
bread which came down from heaven; if any man eat
of this bread he shall live forever."

But while the obligation of typical rites is denied, as
not being essential, or even a proper part of Christianity, they should not be forbidden, if any see fit to use

them according to their original design, in freedom, as illustrations of spiritual things. In teaching the truths of science we are at liberty to employ diagrams, or depend upon verbal descriptions, according to the capacity of the learner. Thus it should be in religion. If the truth can be more forcibly impressed on the mind by dramatic representations, we have the right to employ them : for Christianity, as the final dispensation, the universal religion, is to absorb and utilize all that is valuable in other systems. If, as some think possible, Jerusalem should again be restored, and the Temple rebuilt and refurnished with all its wonderful imagery of the great work of redemption, the knowledge of many might be enriched and their faith strengthened by comparing type with antitype, and seeing the great truths of the Gospel as the apostles first learned to understand the "mystery of godliness."

The plumed dove will not go back to dwell in her nest on the rocks, but she may like occasionally to perch there and see the world as her youth beheld it. For this she should have liberty. "For, brethren, ye have been called unto liberty; only use not liberty for an occasion to the flesh, but by love serve one another. For all the law is fulfilled in one word, even in this, Thou shalt love thy neighbor as thyself." "All things are lawful unto me," said the same great apostle, " but all things are not expedient: all things are lawful for me, but I will not be brought under the power of any." This should be the rule of the Church with regard to all non-essential matters. Whatever is expedient for the present need, whatever will edify a part or the whole, has in this fact sufficient warrant for its use; but so soon as these effects fail, the same law requires its discontinuance, like a medicine that has served its purpose and lost its power from the changed condition of the patient. And if the " old wine " makes the patient's head swim, confusing rather than clearing thought, it is better to change it for the " new wine " of the " Father's Kingdom," that pure love which will never intoxicate;— although "No man having drank old wine straightway desireth new; for, saith he, the old is better."

XIV.

The question of external ordinances, in respect to their obligation and uses, finds pertinent illustration in the Sabbath, which, as a formal and binding statute of the Mosaic dispensation, was abrogated, together with all other symbols of the Law, by the death of Christ, who " took them out of the way, nailing them to his cross." This is sufficiently proved by the fact that Christians changed their day of rest and worship from the seventh to the first day of the week, though all were doubtless at liberty to respect the customs of their fathers who chose to do so: but it was no longer binding on such as had found the substance, which is rest in Christ from our own works.

The dead form of the ritualistic Sabbath was buried with its Lord and raised like him in a freer and more spiritual day of rest and worship known as "the Lord's day." The strictness of restraint was removed, as were the limitations of the body of Christ " made under the law," and yet the essence and virtue of the ordinance remained in a spiritualized form. Christians were no longer subject to the letter which kills, but to the Spirit which gives life.

Such was apparently the design of God respecting everything of an external nature in religion. It is necessary for man, during the period of his tutelage, to have his metes and bounds appointed with exactness, that he may learn, as from the mouth and rod of a school master, the conditions of his being. But as the formal terms of instruction gradually transmute themselves into intelligent principles of conduct, and the key-stone of knowledge is applied, the scaffolding is withdrawn and the arch of life rests on its own foundations. Now Christ was the key-stone of the Jewish dispensation, and the corner stone of the spiritual Temple reared thereon, which is to endure for all ages. In Him the Mosaic law and ritual found a complete transformation. As food taken into the body in gross forms is transmuted by the blood and brain into the substance, or at least the support, of thought and feeling, so in Christ, the living Head of the Church, all the outward ordinances of the first dispensation were changed into spiritual realities. There was once a hidden life in those forms, as there is in articles of food which we consume; and this was sublimated, through the death and resurrection of Christ, to feed and stimulate the heart and brain life of the world; and henceforth the cruder portions of those ordinances became as refuse, and if retained in the living system too long, they burden and ultimately disorder the vital economy. This was conspicuously illustrated in the various reactions which finally brought on the great apostacy, when the whole church seemed given over to form-worship until nominal Christianity became little more than a refined system of idolatry.

It was in view of this inherent weakness and transitoriness of all outward symbols that Paul, as the avaunt courier of the gospel day, warned his Gentile converts to "beware of the concision," to "put no confidence in the flesh." "Ye observe days, and months, and times, and years" was his complaint to the Galatians; "1 am afraid of you lest I have bestowed labor on you in vain." And to the Colossians, "Let no man therefore judge you in meat, or in drink, or in respect of any holy day, or of a new moon, or of a Sabbath, which are a shadow of things to come, but the body is of Christ."

Taking these advices literally the Friends at first rejected the Sabbath, as commonly observed by Christian people, regarding it with all other external ordinances, as a relic of Judaism. They claimed that all days were alike holy to the Christian, and that manual labor when rightly performed for worthy objects, is no less sacred than what are distinctively called religious acts. Therefore, instead of devoting a single day in the week to the cultivation of religion, they met twice in each week for worship, and did not scruple, when their service was over, to resume their business avocations. This they did on "*First-day*," as well as on "Fourth-day."

They were both sincere, and consistent in this radical course; but the storm of opposition raised in the community soon caused the more sensitive to feel that there was a possible mistake—that, as society is built on mutual concessions, one cannot use his liberty to the wounding of a neighbor's tender conscience, without a justifying cause; and that such cause does not exist in the demands of labor; but on the contrary the general need of relaxation and rest affords a sufficient ground for setting apart one day in seven, by common consent, and even by civil statute, for these purposes. And inasmuch as the interests of religion are subserved and protected by the same general order of arrest to business, and to whatever is incompatible with the best uses of the time, the welfare of society—the paramount law—exacts dutiful respect from all to the National Sabbath. They modified their practice, partly out of regard to the feelings of others, though many came to see that important benefits were to be derived from a reasonably close observance of the day of rest, and that serious dangers arise from its neglect and misuse. They have not generally, however, been regarded as good Sabbatarians, and the fact has hurt their influence in many places with other Christian people, and often, probably their laxity in this respect has proved a source of temptation to their children. Regard for the Sabbath has consequently increased among the more thoughtful.

There is no doubt that the Puritan idea of the Sabbath was essentially Jewish, and that laws and usages based on that idea have often been arbitrary and unreasonable. A proper distinction should be drawn between the Jewish and Christian Sabbaths. The difference is of the same character as that between the two religions generally. One was ritualistic, the other realistic. One was a soul encased in a body of flesh and bone; the other is a soul enveloped in a spiritual body. Each has a body, but one binds while it assists growth and development; the other is free, and adapts itself to the situation, obeying the law of an intelligent conscience. One aimed at the establishment of order; the other aims at the promotion of life and happiness. One exhibits the state of childhood, under tutors and rules; the other that of adult manhood governed by recognized principles of propriety and utility. These principles are of equal obligation with fixed laws, and move along similar lines of action, but they admit of greater freedom.

Thus the essential aim of the Sabbatic institution is rest and refreshment for soul and body. Under the Christian dispensation we are not at liberty to disregard the demands of nature, but we are left, with the light of a conspicuous example of Divine wisdom for our instruction, to choose the methods by which we shall reach the desired end. And this we are to do, not for ourselves only, as individuals, but for society as a body. The social body being now in a more advanced condition than formerly admits of more personal liberty; and, judging of this and of the general need, communities have the inherent right to establish such regulations as the general welfare seems to require: and conformity to that order which promotes the best interests of the public is incumbent on every citizen, and especially on every Christian.

XV.

DISCIPLINE.

To some extent every man is his "brother's keeper." God has made us "members one of another," so that kindness and self-love should combine to inspire in each a lively interest in his neighbors' welfare. The closer the relation the greater is the responsibility; and as Christians form a brotherhood, most intimately united, through their common Head, and by an all pervading bond of love, their obligation is very strong, and is rendered doubly imperative by the dangers to which all are exposed.

"Exhort one another daily," says the apostle, "lest any of you be hardened through the deceitfulness of sin." "If any be overtaken in a fault, ye that are spiritual restore such a one in the spirit of meekness, considering thyself, lest thou also be tempted." The right and duty of this brotherly oversight is coextensive with its power to benefit, and is grounded, as we have seen, on the constitution of society. But as the right of every soul to act for itself is also fundamental the good effects of discipline are in the main limited to the persuasive power of love and the "reproofs of instruction." Fear can sometimes be appealed to.

and force may still more rarely be used with wholesome results; but love is the great instrument.

The general principles of Church discipline, as recognized by the Friends are thus stated in the introduction to the Discipline of New York Yearly Meeting.

" It appears by the Holy Scriptures that in the morning of the Gospel dispensation the apostles and believers in Christ met together for the purpose of Divine worship and for the promotion of the cause of righteousness; manifesting a godly care for the preservation one of another, that all might walk by the same rule and mind the same thing, answerable to that precept of our Lord, "One is your Master, even Christ; and all ye are brethren."

" Agreeably to the practice of the primitive Christians we believe it to be our duty, not only to meet together for the worship of God, but also for the exercise of a Christian care over one another, for the preservation of all in unity of faith and practice. For this important end and as an exterior hedge of preservation against the temptations and dangers to which we are exposed, the following Rules of Discipline are adopted for the government of our members and meetings, with the view that in the exercise thereof the unfaithful, and the immoral, and the lifeless professor may be seasonably reminded of his danger and of his duty; and be labored with, in Gospel love, for his help and recovery. When any, by their incon-

sistent or disorderly conduct, have openly manifested
their disunity with the Society it is just and requisite,
that after endeavoring without effect to restore them
the body should testify its disunity with them, at the
same time earnestly desiring that they may be con-
vinced of the error of their ways, and that, through
repentance and a consistent, orderly conduct in future, they may be reunited to us. This being the
utmost extent of our discipline respecting offenders
it is very evident that from the right exercise thereof
no degree of persecution or imposition can be justly
inferred ; for the imposition would rest entirely on
the part of those who might insist on being retained
as members whilst at open variance with the Body,
either in principle or practice."

Then follows an extended description of the order
and purpose of the different meetings, established in
four grades, called Preparative, Monthly, Quarterly
and Yearly Meetings, in which both worship and religious discipline are to be practiced, these constitu-
ting the two general objects of a religious organization.
The system of Friends is extremely simple and democratic. It is intended to be virtually theocratic,
through the administration of Christ as a ruling Head
of the church, not acting through a representative
head, but through each available member of the body
whose judgment and sense of propriety are called upon
to weigh all questions and reach a decision through
what may be termed a *common conscience*. If the

united conscience of the Society, when thus breathed
upon by the Holy Spirit, fails to pronounce with distinctness, the matter is laid over for further reflection
and discussion.

It is difficult to conceive a higher ideal of social administration than this, or one less likely to become
oppressive. It is evidently the system by which
God sought to govern both the Jewish and Christian
churches in earlier times, and is admirable for the security given to justice and for its educating effect on
the people. The only danger lies in the general neglect of duty, and against this no system can guard.
If men become unfaithful and irresponsive to the
motions of the Spirit and the dictates of enlightened
conscience, trouble and declension must inevitably
follow; and the more perfect the machinery for sus-
taining life, the more rapid will be the inroads of disease when any form of evil gains the ascendancy.
This has been painfully illustrated in many instances
by the Friends when traditional ideas of duty took
tho place of living conceptions, and so prevailed in the
general body of the Society that the fresh openings of
the Spirit in a favored few met a cold reception and
had to wait the slow revolution of a mass of minds,
many of which had no wish to revolve at all, thinking
the end of progress had been reached; and so the
Body stood still until death relieved it of its
"weightiest" members, and gradually compelled attention to the causes of injury that were decimating

the Society, or holding it inactive. In this way the system of discipline which was admirably adapted to a morally growing body with a quick and accurate conscience, often became a means of oppression, and a hindrance to its real progress.

Error of any kind having once gained a foothold in such a Society must be difficult to eradicate, because the rule of *unanimity* which the Friends adopted makes it possible for a few influential or obstinate members to put a stop to all action. Experience has proved that the majority rule is in most cases safer, as well as more just; for theoretically all members are equal. and if one be wiser than another he can exert his influence to procure votes for the side he favors. This produces discussion and healthful activity, and is more likely to work necessary changes than the milder method of waiting till all are agreed. There can be little doubt that this peculiar mode of deciding questions by general concurrence in the hope of keeping all united, has done much to reduce the Society of Friends from an intensely radical body, as they were in the beginning, to the most conservative and slow - moving of all the divisions of the Church.

And unfortunately the Discipline when used was too often applied as a pruning hook to rid the Society, not of its immoral and spiritually dead branches merely, but of such as differed on some non-essential matter and chose to assert their liberty thus to differ.

The life of independent thought would thus naturally
be driven from the communion, and those only left
who either had not capacity to think for themselves, or
were too mild in their dispositions to demand reform.
Hundreds and even thousands were disowned for
marrying those not members of the Society ; others
for merely attending marriages where the ceremony
was performed by a " hireling priest." Parents were
disowned for permitting their children thus to follow
the bent of their own inclinations in choosing a partner for life. Others were cut off for attending places
of diversion that were disapproved : others for violat-
ing the law touching " plainness of dress and address," etc., etc.

It is painful to Friends of to-day when this form of
persecution for opinion's sake has finally become almost obsolete, to look back and see the havoc once
made in the Society from these causes. To one who
has not traced the working of those subtle and powerful influences which have poisoned the Church in
all ages, and vitiated its efforts to purify itself by
discipline, it is amazing that a Society like this of the
peaceful and loving Friends could fall into such a pit.
Their misfortune should teach us all to be humble and
extremely cautious in dealing with matters beyond
the clear lines of Christian morality. Even in questions touching important articles of faith it is not the
privilege of nine brothers to exclude the tenth from
the common household because he differs from them,

unless he makes himself offensive by promulgating his opinions too freely. In that case he becomes an aggressor, and may be properly excluded if he cannot be restrained. But when the dispute is about non-essential matters, no right of exclusion exists. The Church of Christ is no man's property ; nor does it belong to any sect, or any number of Christians. We may, if we choose, organize a Reform Association, and invite only those to join who are willing to comply with our rules; but we should not call this the Church of Christ. If we claim to represent the Church, or even a division of it, we have no right to exclude any Christian from its privileges, without a clear Divine warrant. "Who art thou that judgest another man's servant? To his own master he standeth or falleth." Where vital interests are endangered Christ delegates his authority to his ministers, and to the Church as a whole, to preserve order ; but the moment we go beyond the limits of essential truth and morality our commission fails.

It is the besetting sin of disciplinarians to overdo their work. In all ages the Church has suffered from this cause ; and it must be confessed that the Quakers have not proved themselves the happy exception. Their anxiety to present a perfect example to the world has betrayed them into a violation of the rights of private judgment. They have labored to keep their beloved Society clear of all taint of worldliness and error. But alas, like so many before them they have "strained at a gnat and swallowed a camel."

The principal work of discipline must always be accomplished through a lively and efficient ministry. Where the gospel is well preached, and its precepts faithfully applied in the public assemblies, those who refuse the advice thus given will seldom heed more private admonitions. These should not be withheld, where they may do good, and especially where the needful thing had not been said publicly. There is room in the Church for every office of love and kindness, and each member should sympathize and labor with any brother who falls under oppression of the enemy, so long as a chance remains of doing him a service. Only as a last resort is he to be put under restraint, or deprived of his full privileges, in order that he may see his mistakes, and be brought to repentance. The latter course will seldom be found necessary with a real Christian, except when the first symptoms of illness have been neglected, or the wrong treatment given. The proper treatment, and all that will generally be required, is that recommended by the apostle James. "Is any sick among you, let him call for the elders of the Church; and let them pray over him, anointing him with oil in the name of the Lord; and the prayer of faith shall save the sick, and the Lord shall raise him up; and if he have committed sins they shall be forgiven him." If this be effectual, as many believe, for the cure of bodily infirmities, how much more for those of the soul.

But the conditions are important. The true elders are of Christ's appointment, those who have a genuine gift of healing. The oil of brotherly love must be freely applied, as a medium for the grace of God; and prayer must be of the kind that brings the heart of man in such close contact with the Father's heart, that life and renewing warmth are sure to come. Can any soul which is truly born of God long resist such restoratives as these?

If there be any, not "born again from above," who are so unfortunate as to think themselves members of the "mystical body of Christ" because their fathers, or grandfathers, were "grafted in" and became living branches of the Olive tree brought from Heaven, these will resist every appeal to the higher life, simply because they are strangers to it. It is this class which causes the largest amount of trouble in all societies: and if they be close imitations of the true diamond, so that by their respectability they secure positions of honor and influence, the evil is greatly intensified. The struggle becomes almost hopeless when these artificial Christians exert a preponderating influence in the councils of the Church; for having neither eyes to see, nor hearts to feel sympathy for Christ's little ones, they are swayed only by considerations of worldly policy; and their very efficiency, as men of business, hastens the work of destruction. Their wisdom is of that kind which is "foolishness with God." They reason like the chief priests and Pharisees, "If we let this man alone all men will believe on him, and the Romans shall come and take away our place and our nation." Thus the Truth when it does not wear the accustomed livery, and "keep the traditions of the elders," is frowned upon, and, if too persistent, crucified among thieves and robbers. When discipline is thus perverted only revolution and reorganization can effect a cure. Rather than resort to such measures, those among Friends who saw and mourned over the injuries inflicted by hereditary Quakerism remained silent and the sad work of excommunication and repression went on. But the sword has well nigh done its work, and the day-star of liberty, under which all the early victories were gained, seems once more leading the remnant of Israel toward the Land of Promise.

XVI.

"Man in the Fall".—"Original Sin."

On several points of abstract doctrine the Quakers have held views differing more or less from the generally received opinion. As first in order we may consider the effect of "the fall," or Adam's sin, on his posterity. Differences have existed on this and some other points, but probably the most widely accepted opinions are those expressed by Robert Barclay in his celebrated "Apology," to which little, if any, exception was taken during the earlier periods of the Society. In his fourth Proposition, "Concerning Man in the Fall," he says:—

"All Adam's posterity, both Jews and Gentiles, as to the first Adam, or earthly man, is fallen, degenerate, and dead, deprived of the sense or feeling of this inward testimony or seed of God, and is subject unto the power, nature, and seed of the serpent which he soweth in men's hearts while they abide in this natural and corrupted estate: from whence it comes that not only their words and deeds, but all their imaginations are evil perpetually in the sight of God, as proceeding from this depraved and wicked seed. Man therefore, as he is in this state, can know nothing aright: yea, his thoughts and conceptions concerning God and things spiritual, until he be disjoined from this evil seed and united to the *Divine Light*, are unprofitable both to himself and others. Hence are rejected the Socinian and Pelagian errors in exalting a natural light; as also of the Papists and most Protestants who affirm *That man without the true grace of God may be a true minister of the Gospel.*

"Nevertheless, this seed is not imputed to infants until by transgression they actually join themselves therewith; for they are 'by nature the children of wrath' who 'walk according to the power of the prince of the air, the spirit that now worketh in the children of disobedience,' (Eph. 2, 2,) 'having their conversation in the lusts of the flesh, fulfilling the desires of the flesh and of the mind.'"

The two leading points of doctrine above expressed are the *total absence of divine good in man's hereditary nature,* and the *responsibility for that absence.* On the first point Friends do not differ materially from other Christians. On the second they take exception to what is called the doctrine of "Original Sin," by which not only the consequences of Adam's sin are visited upon his posterity, but the sin itself is laid to their account. Lest I should be thought to misstate the case I will quote the carefully prepared definition of the late Dr. Charles Hodge, of Princeton Theological Seminary, in his "Systematic Theology, Vol. II, page 196."

"The Scriptural solution of this fearful problem is that God constituted our first parent the federal head and representative of his race, and placed him on probation not only for himself, but also for all his posterity. Had he retained his integrity, he and all his descendants would have been confirmed in a state of holiness and happiness forever. As he fell from the estate in which he was created they fell with him in his first transgression, so that the penalty of that sin came upon them as well as upon him. Men therefore stood their probation in Adam. As he sinned, his posterity came into the world in a state of sin and condemnation. They are by nature the children of wrath. The evils they suffer are not arbitrary impositions, nor simply the natural consequences of his apostacy, but judicial inflictions. The loss of original righteousness, and the death spiritual and temporal under which they commence their existence are the penalty of Adam's first sin."

Perhaps we cannot do better than listen to Barclay's reply, made two hundred years before, to these remarkable statements.

"I come now to the other part, to wit: That *this evil and corrupted seed is not imputed to infants, until they actually join with it.* For this there is a reason given in the proposition itself, drawn from

Eph. ii, 'For they are by nature children of wrath
who walk according to the prince of the power of the
air, the spirit that now worketh in the children of disobedience.' Here the apostle gives their evil walking,
and not anything that is not reduced to act, as a reason for their being children of wrath. And this is
suitable to the whole strain of the gospel, where no man
is ever threatened or judged for what iniquity he hath
not actually wrought; such indeed as do continue in
iniquity and so do allow the sins of their fathers, God
will visit the iniquity of the fathers upon the children.

"Is it not strange then that men should entertain
an opinion so absurd in itself and so cruel and contrary to the nature as well of God's mercy as justice,
concerning which the Scripture is altogether silent?
: . . This then is not only not authorized by the
Scriptures but contrary to the express tenor of them.
The apostle saith plainly, Rom. iv, 25, ' *Where there
is no law there is no transgression.*' And again, v, 13,
' But sin is not imputed where there is no law.'
Than which testimony there is nothing more positive,
since to infants there is no law, seeing as such they
are utterly incapable of it. . . .

" Secondly, What can be more positive than that of
Ezek. xviii, ' *The soul that sinneth it shall die; the
son shall not bear the iniquity of the father.*' "

When closely pressed the advocates of this strange
doctrine are forced to admit that *guilt* is only a legal
or constructive guilt, like that supposed by the same

system of theology to be imputed by the Divine Father to his son Jesus. Original sin is thus distinguished from actual sin by a line broad enough to make one blameworthy and the other not blameworthy. And this shows that when boiled down the controversy all goes to vapor, "original sin" being nothing but a misnomer for *ungodliness*, or that negative condition to which man descends, with all that pertains to his proper nature, the moment the Spirit of God departs from him. Man in this state is aptly described by the words God addressed to Adam after his transgression; "Dust thou art, and unto dust thou shalt return." All is "of the earth, earthy;" even the marvellous intellect and those genial affections and natural kindness which, in common with lower animals, men, as nobly endowed creatures, imaging the higher glory of heaven, are capable of showing to one another, being only the manifestations of that lower form of life which is fitted to receive the grace and love of God that will raise it to the spiritual plane of being.

While in this "naked" state, that is, unclothed of the higher life of God, man is spiritually dead and incapable of sinning in a strict sense, because the higher law of God has ceased to have dominion over him. This is why Jesus said of the Jews, "If I had not come they had not had sin." The same truth is expressed by the apostle, Rom. vii, 7-9; "I had not known sin but by the law; for I had not known lust

except the law had said Thou shalt not covet. For
without the law sin is dead. For I was alive without
the law once, but when the commandment came sin
revived and I died."

Owing to the poverty of language the word sin is
used to express both the deed and its effects, and the
distinction must be supplied by the mind. Paul en-
deavors to express the distinction by a figure, calling the negative state produced by sin, *dead sin*.
This is but another name for that bondage to self
otherwise called original sin, which is the normal and
universal state of man until the soul is roused to the
consciousness of something higher by the presence
of Christ, first as a moral law and next as a redeeming power of divine love and pity. In both these
characters He appeared to Adam in the garden, after
his fall, and thus revived his defunct moral sense,
and became his Savior by a new birth of God in his
soul.

But this being an engrafted property could not be
transmitted by natural generation to his offspring — a
principle strikingly illustrated in nature by the fact
that the seed of engrafted fruit does not produce the
improved, but only the natural, varieties. Thus the
spiritual nature must be brought forth, or rather added
to, the human nature by that moral inoculation called
regeneration, a work as positive in its character and
effects as natural generation, and doubtless thoroughly analogous thereto, the Spirit of God conveying the

word of salvation, called a'so the Gospel, or grace of
God, to the womb-like understanding of the soul,
where it is either received and embraced by faith,
the soul turning kindly and cordially thereto, or else
is not thus received. On this free and momentous
decision of each individual soul depends the entire
question of its rising to the higher and imperishable
life of God.

Whether this divine life would have accompanied
natural generation if man had not sinned is open to
question, for it appears to have been communicated
to Adam after his physical formation or development had reached a certain stage of mental and moral
susceptibility, fitting him to conceive the idea and
sense of duty. Then God called this primitive form
of moral life into being by giving Adam a command, or law of duty. This law, or Word of God,
contained the germ of spiritual perceptions and relations which generated the conscience, or reflection of the face of God, in the now morally awak-
ened soul. From its nature it would seem that
this effect must in any case have resulted from addresses made to a somewhat advanced understanding, and would therefore be supplementary to the
work of natural generation and growth. In a perfect
being the result would no doubt have been certain,
and the communicated moral life would have passed
from father to child by an easy and normal process
of indoctrination and development, like that now wit-

nessed in what we term healthy moral natures, only in much greater perfection. The effect of sin is to deaden moral sensibility; and this reduced susceptibility to spiritual impressions is no doubt hereditary, and constitutes the great loss which children suffer from their parents' rebellion and immorality, together with the want of that moral seed-sowing which ought to come from the parent to the child.

These results are often cumulative, going on from generation to generation; and this accounts for the wide and rapid spread of evil when once propagated in the rich soil of humanity. As weeds increase faster than the higher order of plants, so selfishness oppresses those finer sentiments which the Spirit of God brings forth in the world, requiring the aid of cultivation to give the latter an equal chance. But there is every reason to believe that the *rewards* of a proper cultivation and improvement of our natural disposition, or moral estate, are shared by our children, as well as the *penalty* of any injury that disposition may suffer through our sinful indulgence. The words *reward* and *penalty* are here used in the qualified sense which gave the name of sin to the hereditary weakness it entails. What is meant is that the effects which the laws of God attach to both good and bad actions are conveyed to posterity as their natural inheritance from those who give them their start in life.

There are those, and some of them are to be found

in the Society of Friends, whose opposition to the doctrine of Original Sin is carried to the extent of denying that any moral taint or infirmity passes from parent to child, each soul being looked upon as a new creation fresh from the hand of God, instead of a new bud on the ever extending vine of a unitary race. This is the other extreme.

To all appearance our mental and moral faculties and propensities bear the features of our parents, and often of our ancestral line for many generations, no less distinctly, than do our physical powers. The entire system of being seems to be modulated and held together by the great law of evolution---the unrolling of the great life current which proceeds from God, first in one, then in several, then in manifold forms and channels, each breaking out again and again in new branches with dividing lines of individual consciousness and will—and so on forever. Nor is there any evidence that the spiritual half of being differs in this respect from that portion which seems, in the largest view, but a grand reflector and exposition of the essential soul-life of the world.

We have before us two opposite conceptions of the soul-life of man, one uniting parent and child so closely that not only the effects, but even the accountability, of personal action passes over from father to son. The other divides them entirely—as much as though their existence began simultaneously on different planets : for the soul is the man, and if this comes immediately from God, unaffected by the channel through which it reaches the world of sense, then the two are not "members one of another," but merely associates in the work of life.

Does not the truth lie between these two theories? The offspring of man is an embryo, not a living soul, until the breath of God, symbolized by the atmosphere of this world, quickens it into a separate personal existence. Then it flashes into conscious being as a joint product of God and man, partaking the attributes of both parental sources. From the human it inherits what we term its lower nature, consisting of such powers and propensities as its earthly parents have to give it. It may be its misfortune that they have nothing better to bestow; but this is the inevitable and just consequences of man's loss of moral, intellectual and physical harmony by sin. God could have slain Adam and made a new father for the race; but He thought best not to do so, preferring to overcome sin and its effects by grace bestowed on each individual of an imperfect race. In a family of free agents sin would be liable to break out at any time and spread its contagion through the whole. It was therefore wiser to let the race be born in the cellar to which the unfaithful husband and wife had fallen, and there receive the first lessons, by fire and candle light; and to such as would accept the invitation, open a stairway up to the light of day, the Father sending down his servants, like the angels Jacob saw,

to bring food and water and give a helping hand, and
finally his ever-faithful Son to reveal to them the perfect law of liberty, and open a still wider doorway
between earth and Heaven.

Those thus born in poverty and filth *seem* to be
treated as though they were guilty of their parents'
sins;—but who that visits the inebriate's den does
not pity the infant there lying on its bed of straw, and
know in his heart that God pities it also, and does
not charge it with its father's crime?

Between each new-born soul and its earthly fountain God interposes, at the moment of awakening consciousness, His superior claim, and says to the aveng-
ing angel, "Spare! As the soul of the father, so also
the soul of the son is mine: The soul that sinneth *it*
shall die." And in due time, even in the midst of
corruption and darkness, there is an unwonted light
in the stable where the kine are feeding, and the Word
of Promise, the Hope of Glory, is laid in the manger
of the hungry heart. Now is its hour of visitation,
its day of grace, big with destiny, when God will undo all the work of evil and call his son out of Egypt,
if in true faith he will keep the commandment of God
to do what is right. Whatsoever the soul thinks to
be right is right for it to do, the *spirit of obedience*, and
not the particular acts performed, being the moral
grace which commends us to God; and this being
the spirit of Christ, whoever does what he believes to
be right, in submission to an overshadowing moral

Authority, whether he call it God or Budda, is breathing in the moral atmosphere of Heaven and entering the higher life of the angelic and divine nature. Thus every soul that recognizes the distinctions of right and wrong and feels urged to do what it thinks to be right is appealed to by God, and empowered by this appeal, to escape from its bondage to self and enter the realm of spiritual life, the paradise of dutiful and loving activity, where Adam walked in the days of his innocence.

The door of entrance from the outside world where we are now born is *Christ on the Cross.* For instead of being easy and natural for us to do right, as would have been the case if our blood had not been drugged by the wine of self indulgence for generations, it is now hard for us to obey the calls of duty. The gate is straight and the way narrow which leads unto this form of life, so contrary to our natural inclinations that it involves, in its complete ascendency, the crossing of all affections and desires which terminate in our personal happiness. Self-love being thus crucified in us, as we follow Christ in the work of regeneration, breathing and walking in his Spirit, the love of God which that Spirit imparts, presently raises the soul from the grave of selfish impulses to the eternal life of God; so that, no longer seeking our happiness apart from God's and that of our fellow-beings, we become united with them in so intimate and harmonious a manner that life and love flow in never ending circles of delight; all that each gives being restored to it with increase by the faithful love of its many friends.

Immortality can thus be seen to result from a life of benignant love and goodness rooted in God; while death as inevitably follows a course of action looking only to self-gratification.   One is a spiral orbit opening outward toward infinity: the other is a spiral orbit closing inward upon itself and ending in the grave, or the hell of unsatisfied desire.

To the choice of these opposite courses every responsible human being is at some time called; and though the number of those who will press through the narrow gateway may always be small, compared with the multitude sweeping on beneath the flowery arch of pleasure into the broad and slippery highway of self-indulgence, the number who reach the better goal is perhaps as great as would be the case if the entrance were made easier.   At all events the conditions of the world are such as men have made for themselves and their offspring, despite God's offered help, all along the ages; and if we perish because we choose that which we know to be wrong we have only ourselves to blame.   The motives to right conduct, and its rewards, are alike increased by the fact that our children and our friends, though not wholly dependent on our integrity for their happiness, are yet profoundly ben fited thereby.   And this great good is attainable only at the risk of their sharing

with us the sad and perhaps fatal consequences of
our fall—fatal not because God judges them for
our fault, but because the imitative property of the
soul, which draws us heavenward in the company of
the good, exposes us likewise to the deadly contagion
of unbelief and sin, and tempts us to drown the "still
small voice" of redeeming love with the clamors of
unhallowed passion and the cries of unsatisfied appetite.

XVII.

JUSTIFICATION—ATONEMENT.

The Friends endeavored to employ language in a way to give distinctness to related ideas. Hence they adopted the primary signification of such words as justification, or *making just*, and atonement, or *making one*, and found much light thrown on these profound questions by this simple use of language. They hold that man cannot be justified while in a sinful state merely by another's doing what is right and throwing the garment of his good deeds, as a screen, over a corrupt heart. God is not thus deceived, however much man may delude himself, and try to make himself appear respectable in borrowed virtue. What is really accomplished is this. When man sins, under stress of temptation, instead of cutting him off, God suffers his love still to flow toward his erring child in a way that diverts attention from his fault, concealing it from the notice of those vindictive sentiments which would exact the immediate and extreme penalty of transgression. This love surrounds the soul that has sinned, just as the blood from a wound in the flesh flows out and covers the wound and forms a protection to it, while the same healing element is at work underneath this covering to supply new flesh and knit together the sundered parts. This act of covering up a wound until the life-building power of love has time to heal the breach of sin, is what is meant by the term justification, in its current theological sense. The idea is that God consents to overlook the injury and treat the sinner as though he were just, until pardoning love, working in the soul, removes the effects of sin and makes it really just, and *at one* with God: that is, until the sin has been atoned for, expiated, blotted out, its divisive force destroyed, and its effects repaired, by the healing power of love.

That such a positive operation takes place every time sin is committed and fully forgiven, any man may convince himself who will watch the operations of his own mind. What is it we do when injured by a friend whom yet we are unwilling to cut off from our regard? Our heart divides itself toward him. One part cries out in indignation against the wrong, while the other pleads for the offender, as the gentler soul of the pitying mother pleads with the sterner, though not less loving, father to remit the sentence due to their child's disobedience. Thus the womanly side of our nature throws the mantle of charity around our sinful friend, and goes to him with the healing balm of its own love; and while entering into judgment with him so tempers judgment with mercy as to work a full reconciliation, or atonement. Now

if we could look in upon our soul during this operation we should see its life-currents flowing forth and
enswathing the soul of our friend, hiding his faults
from the sharp reproaches of our sense of justice,
mitigating his offence, as far as possible, and striving
to revive his languishing affection toward us. If he
accepts our love in a spirit of penitence, and responds
to our kindling warmth, then we altogether bury the
offence, and he becomes to us as though he had not
sinned. He is then justified in a proper sense, his
sin having first been overlooked and finally removed
with all its destructive effects on the harmony of our
united life.

This great work of reconciliation between Himself
and the human race God has effected, and still effects,
by a similar course of action to that we discover in
ourselves under like conditions. It is not perhaps
too much to say that the sin of mankind produces a
divided sentiment in the mind of God towards the
race, constraining him to such variety of purpose and
attitude toward us, in the double character we have
assumed towards Him, as is expressed in the gospel
method of salvation which represents God in the
double character of a vindicator of law and justice
and at the same time a rescuer of men from the fatal
effects of sin; thus in a manner dividing the innermost
soul of goodness, order, truth and love into a du-
al consciousness for the recognition of adverse
claims, and bringing forth a corresponding expression

in the world. This conception of God acting a double part, as Father and Son, while actually one in Spirit, is the ultimate truth of redemption, and the prime mystery of being.

Open as such a revelation must needs be to the scepticism of such as cannot conceive the profounder relations and capacities of spirit-life, doubt is compelled to pause by the discoveries which the human mind is able to make in its own interior world, where a similar dualty and trinity of selfhood is cognizable. Indeed it can be shown that both mental and physical activity depend on such a complex organization. Diversity in unity is the great law of existence. Two, alike and unlike, uniting in and by a third, is the fountain from which the stream of life and all its branches eternally proceeds.

When therefore we listen to those deep utterances which are only the truer because they seem paradoxical, such as, "In the beginning was the Word, and the Word was with God and the Word was God;" "The Word was made flesh and dwelt among men;" "He that hath seen me hath seen the Father;" "I and my Father are one;" "God was in Christ reconciling the world unto Himself," etc., etc.; why should we pronounce them unreasonable when the act by which we judge of them is the result of an organization no less complex and wonderful? For we have not only a soul and body that sometimes work, half with and half against each other, but our body is also double, with two complete sets of organs; and in all probability our soul is equally a dualty, or trinity, of spiritual powers. And these powers of mind and body, though ordinarily working in one line, are capable, in the presence of a disturbing element, of manifesting no little divergence in their inclination and modes of action, amounting not unfrequently to such complete antagonism as to snap the cementing tie which we call Reason, and leave man like a tree split into halves by lightning. This indeed is the natural result of sin, which in its essence is a voluntary discord in the moral attributes of the soul, love of self breaking apart from love of God, to seek its own glory or pleasure. And sin once brought forth casts its shadow, like a dark cloud, or a miasma, far beyond its immediate and responsible source. The effects follow along the invisible cords which unite organ to organ, and soul to soul, even to God Himself, producing everywhere a shadow, or resemblance, of the resulting inharmony, giving to all who are associated in the great bond of unitary life the pain-producing consciousness, or knowledge of evil.

Now this shadow of sin and death, carried up into the mind of God, there produces a semblance of discord and such reversionary action to overcome its effects as has resulted in what is termed the scheme of redemption, that superlative display of Divine love and goodness, in which God takes to Himself the divisive effect of sin, bearing the blow without giving the redound that would carry instant death to the culprit; and sending forth, over the breach of faith, and through the chasm of death, the reviving currents of life and love.

This result is not attained without sacrifice and loss. Justice suffers; Righteousness is wounded and stretched upon a cross; Innocence endures the sorrow which belongs to Guilt; Love reaps what it has not sown, and the Word of God is broken. But at this tremendous cost, Life, the darling of the Father's heart, is saved. And with Life saved, all, or nearly all, the loss can be made up again, by the superlative grace of mercy and the intensified devotion of ransomed spirits.

The life of souls that sin is saved in the same manner as a diseased member of the body is healed, by the remedial action of the nerves and blood distributing the effects of the injury through the system. None of the pain-producing effects of sin are lost. They are only carried into other parts of the system by the law of association which makes vicarious suffering an almost universal experience. This is Love's device for breaking the blow that if unbroken would cut off from the body every wrong doer. But Love does it willing, and by drawing on his creative resources finally fills up the painful breach with renewed joy.

This is the philosophy of the Atonement by which

Christ Jesus, as the embodied representative of the man-ward side of Deity, received the shock of human transgression, and by bearing its pains and returning good for evil, life for death, ransomed the world and reconciled it to God. In so doing he carried the disease, the unrest, the sorrow, and sin, *as represented in its effects*, even to the *appearance* of guilt and blame, or the *shadow* of man's culpability, into his own relations with the Father, *nominally* taking the reproaches of the eternal law of righteousness, with its retributive pains, upon himself, and standing in an *attitude* of hostility to the vindictive purpose of God as the ordainer and upholder of the fundamental relations of right and wrong. . Hence he was permitted to be so borne back into the shades of both physical and moral death, that an awful sense of man's lost condition came upon him, and he cried out under the burden of that vicarious woe and sense of banishment, "My God, my God, why hast thou forsaken me?"

All this was real, and yet the reality of sin and blame was not there. In this crucial vortex, this heart to heart encounter of the incoming tides of sin and death on our side, and the love and faithfulness of God on the other, his body and soul were thrust in twain, earth claiming the lower and heaven the higher part. This fixed, irrefragible grasp of the soul of Jesus on God, amid the agonies of death and separation was the last golden link of the great Atonement which reunited the world of mankind to

God. Love had now conquered sin and death in their most terrible forms.

In all this wonderful work God and Christ are substantially one, one in spirit, purpose and sensibility, even where they are opposed in attitude and appearance. The opposition is dramatic; not a play, but a display of contrary emotions and activities wrought in the ocean of Divine love by the outbreak of sin and the in-pouring of the Amazonian tides of human want and woe. The currents and counter currents of pity and anger are thus set in motion to roll on in majestic unrest until sin and sorrow shall be no more.

Jesus did all things agreeably to his Father's will and commandment. The impulse to save, and the plan of salvation all came from the united heart and mind of Infinite Goodness and Wisdom. All the sufferings of the Son were shared by the loving Father; and the wrath of God against wanton wickedness is expressed in that fearful phrase "the wrath of the Lamb."

It was by virtue of this full and perfect unity while working in apparently opposite, or diverse, directions that the Atonement was effected—or rather *is* effected; for it is, in fact an eternal, continuous, *Process*, needing but once to be exhibited, in histrionic form, but ever, while sin lasts, a profound and palpitating reality.

The *saving virtue* of the Atonement, cannot lie in retributive suffering visited by the Father upon the

Son, as a substitute for the punishment due to man;
because in so doing God would be punishing himself,
and that too for an act of superlative goodness.   This
remarkable conception which maintains its hold with
such singular pertinacity in the popular mind, seems
to have arisen from the close proximity of sin and
suffering, as cause and effect, and from the fact that
the effects of sin pass beyond the individual agent to
those associated with him in the work of life, carrying with them, not the reality, but the appearance of
punishment.   This appearance often gives color to
thought and language, as light passing through a col-
ored medium changes the complexion of objects on
which it falls.   It has thus affected the language of
the Bible.   But when we attempt to convert such ex-
pressions into philosophic terms, without eliminating
the figurative element, the result is a confusion of
ideas.

The simple truth appears to be that when man
sins he wounds not only himself but every part of
the great body of life with which he is united, includ-
ing the Divine Head and Heart whence converge all
the nerves and arteries of this wonderful universe.
And when God consents to give the sinner new life—
that is to forgive his offence—the life sent forth finds
death already in possession of the sinful soul.   When
the Physician comes, therefore, with the sacred fire,
or holy anointing, to kindle anew the extinguished
flame of love, he meets death at the door of the

heart and must press through and overcome his adversary, loosening his grasp by the infusion of new spiritual life, or blood from his own veins. The very nature of deadly sin is that it cuts off the spiritual veins and arteries, called faith, by which the life-blood of one spirit passes to and from another. When restitution is made, these veins and arteries are reunited, or, as we express it in other language, confidence is restored, so that love will flow again from heart to heart, and from member to member. This operation involves a true death, or outpouring of soul life from one to another, in a violent and painful manner, as the blood flows from a wound in the body.

The Atonement is the *making up* between God and man ; and as man has nothing but shame and death to offer, God accepts these and gives life and the position of a claimant to man, Himself bearing the loss, or as we express it figuratively, sharing the penalty, or paying the debt of the guilty party.

We should never have conceived that God really suffers, that His fatherly heart bleeds toward us, every time we sin, if Christ had not come in visible form to make it known to us. Nor could we have imagined that our soul-life is so interwoven with that of God that not only his goodness flows to us, removing our want and pain, but our pains are caught up by the very nerves that bring us relief, and absorbed, and finally extinguished in the infinite heart of God. Thus and thus only can our recovery be effected :

but that which effects the recovery, is not the endurance of pain on God's part, but the *new life and virtue
that come to us in the reviving stream of our Savior's
blood.* The pain is incidental to the healing act; not
a cause, but a consequence; a transferred effect of
sin, deprived in the transfer of the sting of moral
death. By this new outpouring death and the active
power of sin are finally overcome and destroyed as
in a sea of devouring fire, and love and joy reign tri-
umphant.

Such is the great work of human salvation, too
great and wonderful to be expressed in language, or
easily comprehended with all the aids that can be
given. By slow degrees the human understanding, is
expanding to take in its vast proportions. Theory after theory has been proposed, all containing elements of
truth, and probably all of them together insufficient to
exhibit the whole truth. I have tried to follow the
inductive line of what may be termed the Vital Theory of the Atonement, hoping to add a little light to
this most interesting subject of inquiry : I will not say
speculation, because it is as much a matter of science
as any inquiry into the laws and operations of nature ; and the only mystery attaching to it arises from
our inability to penetrate the profound recesses of
our own existence. I have labored to eliminate what
has long been a disturbing factor in the investigation,
namely, the apparent inconsistency attributed to the
Divine conduct in charging the innocent with the

indebtedness of the guilty in satisfaction of the claims
of abstract justice, or in vindication of law, while at
the same time the sentiment of justice demands
that blame shall not be carried over from guilt
to innocence. Even the appearance of so doing
hurts a refined sensibility. The force of association sometimes prevents a proper distinction and
makes a false appearance of complicity with wrong
one of the bitter consequences which innocence has to
bear for guilt. But this arises from men's imperfect
knowledge. When we attempt to carry up the illu-
sion to the mind and heart of God and represent Him
as visiting his righteous displeasure against a sinful
world on the perfect offspring of His own bosom,
in whom He was ever "well pleased," we are going
a step too far.

The hypothesis that Divine justice requires an
atonement for sin in an equivalent of suffering irrespective of the person who suffers, and as a vindication of the authority of law, like a man's paying a debt
for his friend, is founded on one of those half-
truths which are so potent to mislead men of
good judgment. Abstract justice, or the equalizing
of cause and effect, does indeed require that sin shall
be followed by suffering to the full extent of its pain-
producing power. The effect of a blow must lodge
somewhere; and whoever interferes to alter its course
merely diverts the effect from the one on whom it was
about to fall to whatever is put in its place. This

not God Himself can prevent without annihilating
the foundations of life and order.

"All force is twain in one : cause is not cause
Unless effect be there; and action's self
Must needs contain a passive."

The idea of an absolute pardon, or annihilation of
the effects of sin, is therefore baseless. The only
way God can pardon sin is by taking its effects upon
himself and thus excusing the sinner from bearing
them ; and because the effects of certain sins—those
of unbelief, or non-intercourse—will take man to destruction as certainly as the cutting of a branch from
a tree, or a hand from the body, will destroy the
excommunicated member, even death, as one of the
natural effects of sin, must enter into the redemptive process. Christ must needs die—that is he
must become, in a certain manner, separated from
God, which is the essence of death, in order to be in-
corporated with the alien race of man, thus bringing
them new life. " I came forth from the Father and
am come into the world : again I leave the world and
go to the Father."   These are parts of one great act of
self-sacrifice whereby Christ descends into the world
as a man casts himself into the sea to carry a rope to
to a ship-wrecked vessel, and having made fast the line
and bidden the mariners believe in him and follow his
example, returns to shore holding fast the cord, which
represents faith, or the three-fold cable, faith, hope

and love, which binds the world to Heaven.   All this
became indispensable if God would save a lost race ;
and hence, in a certain sense, the great law of justice
called on man's Redeemer to assume man's condition
of suffering and alienation.   Here is the half-truth
which lends to the sufferings and death of Christ the
appearance of a punative satisfaction for man's sin offered by a voluntary partner of his fortunes.

But we all know that no real guilt, except in a certain technical sense of exposure to the retributive
pains of sin, attaches to the character of Christ ; and
hence the language which presents him in that character must all be received as figurative, the apparent
standing for the real truth.

Moreover Justice contains a higher personal element which forbids us to blame the innocent even
when intimately connected with the guilty.   We are
thus compelled to draw a line between sin and that
part of the suffering it causes which is carried beyond
the immediate agent by the corporate ties which
make us all members one of another and of a universal body of life.

Now to say that these sufferings which the innocent
must share with the guilty while they remain together,
and which Christ necessarily assumed with his incarnation, are what satisfies the law of God and expiates the offence of the sinner, is to substitute an effect for a cause.   That which expiates the offence,
atones for the fault, and satisfies the law and mind of

God, is the life and virtue which the innocent bestows
on the guilty in exchange for the sufferings received
from them, and which, by imparting, first a shelter-
ing radiance of reflected light from the good deeds of
him who has espoused their cause, and secondly a
real renovation of life and character to correspond
with the life and character of God, amends the breach
of sin, making full reparation in substituted goodness
and love whose superlative grace atones for past sorrows and fills Heaven and Earth once more with fullness of joy. Sin is thus overcome and its effects
blotted out, and Death and the Grave are despoiled
of their victory unto all who receive the *atoning life*
of the Son of God and are justified in his name, walking in the light of the Lord blameless.

Vicarious suffering is a common, indeed a universal, experience. The innocent are ever suffering with
and for the guilty, bearing their sins and shielding
them from the effects of their errors, by giving them
good for evil, life for death ; just as the sound members of the body share the restraints and pains of the
unsound, and atone for their defects by sending them
new blood and nerve force to overcome their disorders. And it is a glorious truth that the Head and
Heart of all being originate and sustain this great
work of salvation, causing all the members to participate therein according to the need ; and that only
thus can erring man live for a day, by feeding on the
substituted life of God, the " flesh and blood "of re-

deeming goodness and love, brought to him in the Word of reconciliation, "the Son and sent of the Father," the person, Christ Jesus—for *all God's life is personal when embodied in definite conceptions and forms.* And that God, as a true Father, so shares our sorrows and enters into our woes, and gathers up in his almighty hand the seeds of death and destruction, consuming them in the fires of his love, that our life is renewed within us day by day, and moment by moment. As the breath of heaven enters our lungs to impart new energy to our blood and at the same time snatch away its impurities which contain the seeds of death, and as food and water enter our bodies to carry on the same great work of ministration to our soul-life, so the Word and Spirit of God are ever at work, replenishing, purifying, energizing our spiritual natures, and bearing away the effects of our sins together with the ashes of our spent vitality.

The incarnation and death of Christ, which are parts of one act, brought these eternal truths within the horizon of man's knowledge in a way most profoundly to impress the sensitive mind with a conception of God's pitying love, and thus engender returning love, and awaken sorrow for sin by showing its sad effects. The sufferings of Christ Jesus thus become the exponent and measure of God's love for his erring children, and contribute to the work of atonement by their stimulating influence on the sinner's mind, and as well, no doubt, by their softening and tendering effect on the mind of God, considered as standing aloof from man on the ground of abstract justice, but now, by a fellow feeling of pain stimulated to pity and a new and superlative out-pouring of love, as of blood going forth from the wounded heart to cover up, and finally obliterate both sin and its consequences.

It is of vast importance that these moral effects of Christ's death and sufferings should not be lost, as they form the kindling torch in the hand of the evan-gelist with which he must set fire to the dead human heart and conscience. Hence the vigilant jealousy with which the evangelical Church guards the doc-trine of the Atonement in its popularized forms of statement, because these give a flesh and blood pic-ture of the saving love of God for lost humanity, a picture which takes hold, as no philosophic state-ment can do, of the heart and emotions, working through the imagination to beget a likeness of Christ in the soul. And this is why God presented that wondrous life-portrait of himself to the world, that man might be captured by it, and caught up in-to such an enthusiasm of admiration that he would take on the stamp of a new and higher life. This ardor and glow of loving enthusiasm, circling about the folds of the excited imagination is what effects the new birth, Christ within, the hope of glory, the em-bryo angel of an immortal existence. Better far that

the imagination should be overwrought and embrace
some errors of judgment, than that it should not
warm to the saving conception of God's infinite love
in sending his Son to live and suffer and die, that we
poor sinners may live forever, taking on himself the
insufferable burden of our woes, and giving us life
and joy instead, out of his abounding fullness. If by
a stretch of the imagination we can also cast off our
stifling and appalling sense of guilt on our mighty
Sponsor and let him carry it away, as a scapegoat
into the wilderness, we are then well rid of it, and
shall have time enough by and by to learn that this
part of the transfer was only an appearance, a shadow,
wherein we seemed to see our Substitute going off
under the frown and lash of Divine justice, leaving
us the fleece and skin of his own righteousness with
which to cover our nakedness. All this may sometimes be needful to the heart's rest from its taunting
convictions of guilt, in that state of unreason when
appearances have all the force of facts. And yet to
set it down in the books, and offer it, in cool reason,
to men of understanding, as theologically true, and
an essential part, yes the very foundation stone, of
the scheme of human salvation, is carrying matters
quite too far, and is beginning to react against the
claims of Christianity in many thinking minds. The
world is growing more thoughtful and analytic in its
reception of religious as well as other truths, and we
must consider the intellect as well as the heart. We

must not repel the strong man from the church in order that it may be filled with women and children, or those whose faith does not demand logical consistency. Christianity contains no more fiction than we ourselves attach to it; and though it is able to bear up, and do its life-saving work, under many encumbrances, the less we wreathe the sword with the dry leaves, of imagination, the keener will be its edge.

Perhaps it would not be right to offer the above, as the expressed Quaker doctrine of the Atonement; for they have never formulated any definite statement of this particular doctrine, and have always been more or less divided with regard to it; some holding what is known as the orthodox theory, in one or another of its many phases, and others rejecting the whole on account of the difficulties I have pointed out. I think however that what is here advanced belongs naturally to their general system, which rests on the substantial work of religion in the soul, making all our relations to God positive and vital, and viewing the external work, even of Christ himself, as a glorious display, in living, and historic, and heart-inspiring vision, of the world-wide and eternal verities of our inner life.

The doctrine above defined may be summarized thus:

Man's justification and atonement with God rest not on the *imputed*, but on the *transmitted* and *vitally inwrought*, grace and righteousness of Christ, whose incarnation, life, death, resurrection, ascension, and return in the Spirit, are the symbol and supreme instrument of such transfer and reconciliation.

With this we may compare a few passages showing how the Quakers have reviewed the matter.

——"As many as resist not this *light* but receive the same, it becomes in them a holy, pure and spiritual birth, bringing forth holiness, righteousness, purity, and all those other blessed fruits which are acceptable to God : by which holy birth, to wit, *Jesus Christ formed within us,* and working his works in us, as we are sanctified, so are we justified in the sight of God, according to the Apostle's words : " But ye are washed, but ye are sanctified, but ye are justified in the name of the Lord Jesus, and by the Spirit of our God." I Cor. vi, 2.   Therefore it is not by our works wrought in our own will, nor yet by good works considered as of themselves; but by *Christ,* who is both the *gift* and the *giver,* and the cause producing the effects in us ; who, as he hath reconciled us while we were enemies, doth also in his wisdom save us and justify us after this manner, as saith the same Apostle elsewhere : 'According to his mercy he saved us, by the washing of regeneration, and the renewing of the Holy Ghost.'"   Tit. iii, 5.

Apology, Prop. VII.

"The state of the controversy being thus laid down,

these following positions do from hence arise in the next place to be proved.

"First, that the obedience, sufferings, and death of Christ is that by which the soul obtains remission of sins, and is the procuring cause of that grace by whose inward workings Christ comes to be formed inwardly, and the soul to be made conformable unto him, and so just, and justified.

"Secondly, That it is by this inward birth of Christ in man that he is made just, and therefore so account-ed of God: wherefore, to be plain, we are thereby, and not till that be brought forth in us, *formally*, if we must use that word, justified in the sight of God.

"Thirdly, That as *good works* as naturally follow from this birth as heat from fire, therefore are they of *absolute necessity to justification*, as *Causa sine qua non*, i. e. though not as the cause *for which*, yet as that *in which* we are, and without which we cannot be, justified."

—Ibid, § IV.

(Good works are here defined, by a happy illustra-tion, so as to include the first fruits of the new life, the right affections of the soul.)

"They object, verse 21st of the same chapter (2 Cor. v.) 'For he hath made him to be sin for us who knew no sin, that we might be made the righteousness of God in him.' From whence they argue That as our

JUSTIFICATION—ATONEMENT   163

sin is imputed to Christ, who had no sin; so Christ's
righteousness is imputed to us, without our being
righteous.

"But this interpretation is easily rejected; for
though Christ *bare our sins*, and *suffered for us*, and
was among men *accounted a sinner*, and numbered
among transgressors; yet that God reputed him a
sinner is nowhere proved. For it is said, He was
found before him *holy, blameless* and *undefiled*, neither was there found any guile in his mouth. That
we deserved those things, and much more, for our
sins, which he endured in obedience to the Father,
and according to his counsel, is true; but that ever
God reputed him a sinner is denied: neither did he
ever die that we should be reputed righteous, though
no more really such than he was a sinner, as here-
after appears. For indeed if this argument hold it
might be stretched to that length as to be very pleasing to wicked men that love to abide in their sins: for
if we be made righteous as Christ was made a sinner,
merely by imputation, then as there was no sin, not
the least, in Christ, so it would follow that there needed no more righteousness, no more holiness, no more
inward sanctification in us than there was sin in him!
So then by his *being made sin for us* must be understood his *suffering for our sins* that we might be made
partakers of the grace purchased by him, by the
workings whereof we are made the righteousness of
God in him. For that the Apostle understood here

a being made really righteous and not merely being reputed such, appears by what follows, seeing in in verses 14, 15, 16, of the following chapter he argues largely against any supposed *agreement of light and darkness, righteousness and unrighteousness;* which must needs be admitted if men are to be reckoned ingrafted in Christ, and real members of him, merely by an imputative righteousness wholly without them, while they themselves are actually unrighteous. And indeed it may be thought strange how some men have made this so fundamental an article of their faith which is so contrary to the whole strain of the gospel: a thing which Christ in none of all his sermons and gracious speeches ever willed any to rely upon, recommending to us works, as instrumental in our justification. And the more it is to be admired at, because that sentence or term so frequently in their mouths, and so often pressed by them as the very *basis* of their hope and confidence, to wit, The imputed righteousness of Christ, is not to be found in all the Bible, at least to my observation.

Ibid. § *VI.*

XVIII.

The Friends early advocated the doctrine of man's moral perfectibility in this life. They believed that Christ set no unattainable standard before His disciples—that when He commanded them, "Be ye perfect, even as your Father who is in Heaven is perfect," He intended, and was able, to furnish them with sufficient grace fully to overcome sin. Not that they were to be soon made infallible. There is a difference between sinlessness and infallibility. Adam was for a time sinless, but was too weak to withstand his wife's persuasions, added to those of the serpent. Job was strong enough for that, but sank into distrust of God under the long continued strain of bereavement and intense bodily suffering. Doubtless there have been many whose hearts were thoroughly cleansed of all impure affections and motives, who were yet sometimes thrown from their foundation by sudden fear, or strong appeals to their natural propensities—those motive forces without which man would be unqualified for his work in this world. Cleared of this misconception the doctrine of Perfection, or Holiness, as it is now called, is highly commendable to the earnest believers in it; for it exalts the power of redeeming grace, gives vigor and directness to faith, and emphasizes the demands of God's righteous law upon us. If God has given laws to men which they cannot obey He is merely playing with them. This is insupposable. Such an assumption gives a dangerous license to sin, and puts a fearful weapon into the hands of the Tempter.

We are called to holiness of heart and life, and are not at liberty to say, " When we have done with this world, which was made for sinners, then we will lead holy lives." How do we know there are not plenty of these procrastinating sinners in the other world? The probability would seem to be that it is full of them. What is there about death that is capable of transforming a sinner into a saint? If we put off our flesh and bones does that necessarily relieve us of a desire to seek our own happiness irrespective of the wants of others? The root of all sin lies here, and this is a fault of the soul, not of the body. Our bodily wants intensify the strain upon us to seek satisfaction and relief in a selfish way; but many of our sins have little to do with the body. What has the love of fame, of admiration, of social preferment, to do with this life that it may not with a life of pure mentality? Selfishness only takes a more refined type in the intellectual ranks of being: and nothing but the love of God can overcome this root of iniquity in man or angel.

Nor can any reason be seen why that grace which is able to transform savages into men may not so entirely master our selfish impulses as to elevate men into saints before they leave this world. Indeed this world is just the place for saints—where they are most needed and can do most honor to their Lord and King. Why is Jesus called the King of saints if He has not one in his train, or in all his earthly province? Unhappy sovereign, to rule over a nation of hypocrites; for if Christians are not, much of their time, free from impure and selfish desires—if they do not, out of a clean heart, love God and their fellow men as much as they love themselves, then they are mere pretenders, for this is what the law of God imperatively demands. And though a man cannot gain this of himself; though for a long time the flesh will war against the spirit and the spirit against the flesh; though we must again and again cry out " Who shall deliver me from the body of this death? " he who perseveres in wrestling prayer and prayerful wrestling, as did the zealous patriarch and apostle, will at length break forth in song with him, " I thank God through Jesus Christ our Lord." And though at this time, while under a load of physical infirmity which cramped and chained his soul to the things of sense, he could find comfort only in dividing himself in two parts, he ceased not to "press toward the mark for the prize of the high calling of God in Christ Jesus." And before his close he could say " I have fought the good fight,

I have finished my course; I have kept the faith, henceforth there is laid up for me a crown of righteousness which the Lord, the righteous Judge, shall give me at that day : and not to me only, but to all them also that love His appearing."

"Though I affirm," says Barclay, "that after a man hath arrived at such a state in which he may be able not to sin, yet he may sin; nevertheless I will not affirm that a state is not attainable in this life in which to do righteousness may be so natural to the regenerate soul that in the stability of that condition he cannot sin."

Have we not all known good fathers, and especially good mothers, from whose hearts every trace of real selfishness was gone? They themselves may feel that they are impure, because gross nature has its demands. They would like to dissolve into pure air or sunlight, and go like Jesus to be the life of the world. But we are quite willing they should preserve their individual marks, and even bear a load of flesh somewhat longer. Nor will we charge them with sin, or any shade of moral imperfection, because their personal preservation necessitates an occasional thought for themselves. Even should their sense of justice prove so vigorous as at times to break out in holy indignation against wanton wrong, we would not reduce their crown by a single star; for so did not His, who to the tenderness of a woman and the meekness of a saint, added the fire of an angel and the indignation of God? Holiness is *wholeness*, and though the conception opens a long road to progress when applied to the entire being, body, soul, and mind, in the sense of sinless cleanness of heart and purpose, it should be the crown of every Christian life. Let "*Holiness to the Lord*" be inscribed in golden letters over every church door, and on the shield of every Christian warrior: and though the dust of battle may sometimes obscure its brightness, let none remove the sacred pledge of a heavenly inheritance, but as speedily as possible burnish it again in the fire of a Savior's love.

Perseverance is necessary both to reach and to maintain Perfection. Life rests, and will always rest, on free and right volition. The free volitions of God are the fountain out of which all things flow, and the soul that is created in God's likeness will never be encased in a shell, or live in a city whose gates are not open to ingress and egress for its free-born citizens. Every "decree of election" is conditioned on this fundamental law of existence. We say God can do no wrong, for we can conceive of no possible motive for wrong conduct where perfect intelligence combines with infinite power and goodness. The necessary ignorance and inexperience of new-born finite minds exposes them to temptation. In its early searches for happiness the soul may easily be misled; and until the moral protoplasm of kindly impulses is organized and confirmed by acts of intelligent good-will into virtuous character, the desire to please one's self, or those making the latest appeal, may readily vitiate our relations with those to whom constant affection is due.   This general condition of finite being causes the need of a state of probation for the development of character.   But as good impulses and intelligence grow together, the mind gradually rises out of the mysteries which envelop its birth and childhood into the clear atmosphere of perfect knowledge: and when the soul has not only become purified, but is also filled with the love of God, as a house is filled with summer light and warmth, and has become fully informed of all the circumstances of its being, and is fully and habitually disposed to do good, then it has reached a state like that of God Himself, where to sin is impossible, while yet its acts are freely virtuous.

This kind of freedom differs from that where a soul can elect to do good or evil, as is the case during its probation.   As we go on making good or bad choices, these choices finally build up a framework of solid character which impedes our progress backward, leaving us only the modified liberty of moving in the direction we have chosen, be it right or wrong.   This appears to be a general law of life.   For illustration take the formation of the earth itself, which during its gaseous and liquid stages may be supposed to have chosen its own form and arranged its materials to suit itself.   But by slow degrees it hardened into a solid framework of continents. Gradually the sea-line of liberty receded within smaller limits, and ultimately it will cease altogether. So with every other known form of life, Even the human soul, at first so plastic, in a few years becomes like the solid rock for consistency of character. This fearful and yet blessed law of continuity sets the stamp of eternity on all the works of God which please Him. But He has not resigned His power to dissolve and make over those forms of life which displease Him. In this benign work of dissolution and recreation God is constantly employed, and will be so while imperfection and sin exist.

To what extent a genuine work of grace may proceed without producing a fixed character seems very uncertain. Some think this whole question is determined by Divine election; that every one who experiences the new birth will certainly be saved, being recovered from every fall, or mis-step, by the effectual grace of God. If this be admitted the question will then arise What constitutes this new birth? for it seems quite certain that many are visited by redeeming grace and quickened to a considerable degree who afterwards fall away and end life in darkness. Paul evidently felt it possible for himself to become a "castaway" after having preached to others and "done many wonderful works." Many passages of Scripture prove the same truth, and, receiving these in their plain import, the Friends have always urged the necessity of persevering unto the end, in the spirit of the promise, "Be thou faithful unto death and I will give thee a crown of life."

As "many are called but few chosen," it would seem that the glorious estate of sonship is not fully conferred on man until by a settled and determinate bent, not only of will but of a nature pretty well redeemed from sin, preparation has been made for the final adoption and seal of the Spirit. Then the soul is wedded to Christ by an inseparable bond, and will grow up with Him into all perfections of faith, hope, knowledge and love.

"Unto every one of us is given grace according to the measure of the gift of Christ. Wherefore he saith When He ascended up on high he led captivity captive and gave gifts unto men. . . . And He gave some apostles, and some prophets, and some evangelists, and some pastors and teachers; for the perfecting of the saints, for the word of the ministry, for the edifying of the body of Christ; till we all come, in the unity of the faith, and of the knowledge of the Son of God unto a perfect man, unto the measure of the stature of the fullness of Christ."—Eph. iv, 7-13.

XIX.

But a very small proportion of the Society of
Friends have ever denied the Divinity of Christ.
Some have held the doctrine in an unorthodox form,
speaking of Christ, in his spiritual being, as an ema-
nation, or attribute, of God, rather than as a Divine
Person. But even these are free to admit that what
gave Jesus his power and glory was a real birth of
God, and that this made him the Son of God in a
proper sense. The ultra-unitarian element, however,
are inclined to extend the title equally to all who receive the "Holy Anointing" which made Jesus a Son,
or, as they distinguish Him, an "elder brother." In
vindication of their view they refer to various expres-
sions of the Lord Himself, as where He said to Mary,
on the morning of his resurrection, "Go to my brethren and say unto them, I ascend unto my Father and
your Father, and to my God and your God." There
can be no doubt that a glorious truth is here, as elsewhere, plainly taught. For if Jesus be "the Vine"
and His disciples "the branches," they too are sons
of God in a proper sense.

But the question here takes a higher range, and inquires whether there be a difference in *kind*, or *quality*, of relationship, as well as in degree of nearness to the common Father. Was the Divine Life which united with the seed of the Virgin the same as that which unites with the moral germ of kindly desires in the human soul when a "new creature" is generated and man becomes a Christian? or was it the pre-existent Son of God in Heaven who thus took upon Himself the form and frame of our degenerate Humanity that He might lift it, by the quickening embrace of God, to a position of pardon and safety? The latter is the approved orthodox theory; or rather doctrine; for few are so bold as to attempt theorizing on matters of such magnitude and difficulty. Wherever this has been attempted the failure to adapt such mighty problems to human comprehension has been conspicuous. Nor does it seem worth our while to quarrel about things in their nature inexplicable so long as the Scriptures are not denied and the practical duties and relations of life are tolerably well agreed upon.

It is perhaps no easier to explain how a Christian is born of " the incorruptible seed and Word of God," than how an already conscious spirit could assume special connections with a more material form of life.

So far as we can understand, God is always incarnating Himself in the various forms and powers of nature to create new centers of vital activity. These new centers of positive and reflex action form the beginnings of soul life. And it was to inaugurate a new system of moral and spiritual activities that the creative Word of God closed in with the alienated world of mankind and sent forth from Bethlehem and Calvary a stream of Divine glory that should regenerate and evermore uplift the race. How it was done no man can tell—perhaps not the angels; and yet it may have been as simple and natural as any other act of Divine power and wisdom. We see the result, and know that God has been walking amongst us—that He, even the Eternal One, has taken us by the hand, and is lifting us up, and washing away our sins in His own pure life. We know that miracles are wrought, more wonderful than the destruction of armies, the dividing of seas, and the shaking of mountains—miracles of life and salvation, healing the the sick and raising the dead. All this we see with our own eyes, and our own hearts tell us. We know that we have passed from death unto life, and that we have looked upon the Son of God, for His light enlightens our eyes and the warmth of His love inspires our hearts.

And when this new life is fully ours we shall not cry Anathema against a brother who differs somewhat from ourselves in his apprehension of the method and philosophy of Christ's redemptive work.

Friends did not set out to become theologians. Their religion was eminently practical at first and has largely remained so. As a rule they accepted

the statements of the Bible without questioning, and
were generally able to harmonize apparently incongruous passages by appealing to the "spirit which
gives life," rather than to the "letter which kills."
At the rise of the Society they were accused of holding unitarian doctrines. This they did not deny in
the sense of believing in one God, rather than three
Gods. But in this they went no farther than the most
intelligent Trinitarians now do. What they opposed
was Tritheism, or that extreme of Trinitarianism
which makes the deity "subsist in *three distinct and
separate persons.*" No well-informed theologian will
now maintain the *separate* existence, or subsistence,
of Father, Son, and Spirit, but rather their entire
unity in one substance, will, and purpose. Such was
not the view, however, of the ignorant clergy of the
seventeenth century who could not understand the
Articles of their own Church. It was to refute their
crude notions of this and other doctrines that William Penn, on being denied a public hearing by a
clergyman who had accused him of unsoundness,
wrote "The Sandy Foundation Shaken, or those so
generally believed and applauded doctrines of one
God subsisting in three distinct and separate persons; the impossibility of God's pardoning sinners
without a plenary satisfaction; the justification of
impure persons by an imputative righteousness, re-
futed from the authority of Scripture testimonies and
right reason."

In this work, which cost the youthful hero his liberty, Penn says: "Mistake me not: we never have disowned a Father, Word and Spirit, which are ONE; but men's inventions: For, 1. Their *Trinity* has not so much as a foundation in the Scripture. 2. Its original was three hundred years after Christianity was in the world. 3. It having cost much blood, in the council of Sirmium, Anno 355, it was decreed, *that thenceforth the controversy should not be remembered, because the Scriptures of God make no mention thereof.* Why then should it be mentioned now with a *Maranatha* on all who will not bow to this abstruse opinion? 4. And it doubtless hath occasioned idolatry: witness the popish images of Father, Son, and Holy Ghost. 5. It scandalizeth Turks, Jews and Infidels, and palpably obstructs their reception of the Christian doctrine. Nor is there any more to be said on behalf of the other two: for I can boldly challenge any person to give me one Scripture phrase which does approach the *doctrine of satisfaction* (much less the name) considering to what degree it is stretched : not that we do deny, but readily confess, that Jesus Christ, in life, doctrine and death, fulfilled his Father's will and offered up a most satisfactory sacrifice ; but not to pay God, or help him (as being otherwise unable) to save men; and for a justification by an *imputative righteousness* whilst not real, it's merely an imagination, not a reality, and therefore rejected; otherwise (if a real righteousness) confest and known

to be justifying before God, because *there is no abiding in Christ's love without keeping his commandments.*"
        —Janney's Life of Penn, page 54.

It is unnecessary to repeat what has before been
said, in the chapter on Justification and Atonement,
on the last two topics of the above extract. And to
show that the position assumed on the question of
Tritheism, was not different from that of orthodox
theology at the present time, I will present a few ex-
tracts from Dr. Hodge's Systematic Theology, Vol. 1.,
page 460.

The Mutual Relations of the Persons of the Trinity.

"On this subject the Nicene doctrine includes:

"1.   The principle of the subordination of the Son
to the Father, and of the Spirit to Father and Son;
But this subordination does not imply inferiority.
For as the same divine essence with all its infinite
perfections is common to the Father, Son, and Spirit,
there can be no inferiority of one person to the other
in the Trinity.   Neither does it imply posteriority; for
the divine essence common to the several persons is
self-existent and eternal.   The subordination intended is only that which concerns the mode of subsistence and operation, implied in the Scriptural facts
that the Son is of the Father, and the Spirit of the
Father and Son, and that the Father operates through
the Son, and the Father and Son through the Spirit.

"2. The several persons of the Trinity are distinguished by a certain 'property,' as it is called, or characteristic. That characteristic is expressed by their distinctive appellations. The first person is characterized as Father, in his relation to the second person; the second is characterized as Son, in relation to the first person; and the third as Spirit, in relation to the first and second persons. Paternity, therefore, is the distinguishing property of the Father; filiation of the Son; and procession of the Spirit. It will be observed that no attempt at explanation of these relations is given in those ecumenical creeds, namely, the Nicene, that of Constantinople, and the Athanasian. The mere facts as revealed in Scripture are affirmed.

"3. The third point decided concerning the relation of the persons of the Trinity, one to the other, relates to their union. As the essence of the Godhead is common to the several persons, they have a common intelligence, will, and power. There are not in God three intelligences, three wills, three efficiencies. The three are one God, and therefore have one mind and will."

It can easily be seen how far such language falls short of describing a "God subsisting in three distinct and *separate* persons." Inexplicable as the subject must necessarily be, like all others where there is an organic union of various elements, (as of soul, body and mind in one being called man,) we can yet perceive that the moment separation takes place, unity ceases. This is what deepens the mystery of the incarnation into almost absolute darkness; for there we behold the Son *apparently* separated from the Father so as to display a distinct will—"not my will but thy will be done." And yet in this very utterance Jesus manifestly divides his own will in two, one part of which coincides with his Father's will, while the other, originating in his human soul, and really but an impulse, urges for relief, but is firmly held in subjection to that part of his nature which corresponds with the nature and mind of his Father. Nor is there any dealing with the life of this "Immanuel" except on the supposition that two natures, or related systems of vital force, combined in him, as sunlight combines with air, earth or water to give life to the otherwise barren world.

We only betray our ignorance when we attempt to deny that such corporate unions of kindred but diverse elements are possible to spirit as well as matter; for all vital action is the result of such combinations. And seeing that nature, from crystal up to man, is but a vast concatenation of forms and forces whose vitality and efficiency depend on inscrutable marriage relations, filial evolutions and involutions, and eternal processions and reunions, where shall we look for the archetype of all this beauteous wonder-world if not in the infinite Father and Fountain of being?

To suppose that the source of all the varied forms

in the universe is itself a simple essence without a constitution adapted to manifold methods of vital activity is to fail in the first step toward an orderly conception of life. If like begets like the world He has made must resemble God, and we have only to read correctly the lessons He has placed before us in Nature and in ourselves in order to understand the nature of Him who, while He is truly *one*, by the eternal "beginnings" of life and action becomes a *two-one* and a *three-one* and an *Infinite-One*. "As Thou, Father, art in me, and I in Thee that they also may be one in us."

But I may not pursue the theme here, my object being to show that in the light which rose with unwonted clearness on their minds the early Friends, while not beyond mistakes, and, as Paul confessed for himself and others, knowing only "in part," they were to a remarkable extent brought near the medium line of rational Christian truth. In later days some have deviated each way from the primitive faith, as will appear in another chapter.

XX.

Friends have never believed in the literal resurrection of the body. They believe that it is God's design to renovate the souls, and even the bodies, of those whose faith is sufficient, so that the entire manhood shall be raised from the death of sin, and made to stand before God in the beauty of holiness. The resurrection of the body of Jesus was a type of this transformation and uplifting of even our physical nature from its bondage to the elements of this world into an instrument of happiness and power. But it does not appear to have been the design of God in our creation to fix the relations of the intelligent spirit to matter so that it should never pass on from a cruder to a finer form. No reasonable view of the history of life on this planet would lead us to suppose that had man remained innocent his "earthly house of this tabernacle," would forever have retained its heaven-born occupant. Nor would it have been a fit companion for him in his endless progress Godward.

The apostle Paul seems clearly to have understood the case by that fine inspiration which enabled him

to anticipate by two thousand years many of the discoveries of slow-paced Science. He shows that a
"spiritual body" succeeds to the "natural body"
somewhat as the light aerial blade of wheat rises
from the matured and solid grain. The image is a
beautiful one. In each there is a living germ, imperishable while it keeps the law of life, and a sur-
rounding frame which gives it form and connection
with the world of nature. To those planted here in the
dark soil of earth, the life seems to become lost, swallowed up of death and corruption ; but just above,
bright with a new and vernal birth, waving its wings
in the open sunlight and the fresh airs of heaven, the
rising angel of the hidden life puts on its glorious
apparel and stands, fluttering with youthful delight
in the presence of the benignant Sun.

True is it that the natural body helps to endow the
new angelic manhood. How, we cannot tell. The
memories of our earthly life will cling to us, and the
love of our friends will still be a part of our heavenly
existence. Perhaps an ethereal form will issue from
the dying frame. But all transpires in a natural order of progression. The wheat does not come back,
days afterward, and take up bodily the grain that was
buried in the soil. Neither will the soul of man thus
return to uplift the handful of ashes that remains
where its tabernacle is consumed. This is the dream
of imagination, the poetry of the world's childhood,
the symbolism of oriental philosophy, and not the

sober truth of Science and Revelation. But until the
mind of the race grows strong enough to perceive
truth in its higher forms it is useless to try to draw
it from the emblems which stand to it for realities.
The plainest words cannot convey ideas until the intellect is able to receive them. Religious development
has its period, corresponding to our toy-loving childhood, when images, like waxen dolls, are as dear to us as
the solid verities of life ; even more so. But when we
become men, like Paul, we shall " put away childish
things " of our own accord.

It will seem irreverent to many to say that the anticipated Second Coming of Christ in an outward,
visible, and even physical form (for the doctrine is
that he still occupies the same body which he raised
from the grave,) is one of those illusions of our religious childhood which are to be outgrown. That even
the apostles entertained and cherished it proves
nothing, only that the time had not then come when
the disciples could bear the naked truth. "I have
yet many things to say unto you but *ye cannot bear
them now*. Howbeit, when he, the *Spirit of Truth* is
come, he will guide you into all truth : for he shall
not speak of himself; but whatsoever he shall hear
that shall he speak : and he will show you things to
come. He shall glorify me : for he shall receive of
mine and shall show it unto you." This is saying
plainly that all truth was not to be revealed at once

to those who represented the Church of Christ.
They were to come gradually to a clear apprehension
of the *spirit* of truth. They had its emblematic
forms, just as they had Christ in a body of flesh before them. But he declared to them, "It is expedient for you that I go away: for if I go not away the
Comforter (the Spirit of truth) will not come unto
you; but if I depart I will send him unto you. And
when he is come he will reprove the world of sin, and
of righteousness, (that which is righteous in form but
not in spirit) and of judgment" (judgment that is literal and false also in spirit). Then, after the passage
first quoted above, in which he states that he has yet
many things to say to them which they are at present
unable to bear, he adds, "A little while, and ye shall
not see me, and again a little while and ye shall see
me, because I go to the Father." How plain it is
that his return, or second coming, was to be, not in
physical form—for why should he bring back to the
world that which was already operating as a veil to
his disciples' minds? —but in spirit and truth. And
when he did thus return, according to his promise
in "a little while,"—not after many centuries—his
disciples all recognized him, with their proper mental
organs, in that substantial and eternal and glorious
form in which he is, and will ever remain, a Sun to
the moral and spiritual firmament of this now rapid-
ly awakening world.

The change which will make him ever more and

more clearly visible to mankind, is to take place not
in him, but in ourselves as the spiritual faculties of
the race gradually become perfected, and our mental
eyes throw off the scales of a sometime useful but
now blinding formalism, and learn to see "the Way,
the Truth, and the Life" of God in his beautiful and
glorious simplicity. We shall then also be able to
recognize the angels and saints who come with him
in their "celestial bodies" to judge the world and
raise it from the long sleep of death in which unbelief has steeped its finer senses.

That both Christ and his saints and angels have bodies so far kindred to matter that they can affect our
physical organisms, and even what seem to us the
"blind forces of nature," is highly probable, indeed
necessary to any intelligent working system of unitary life in the world. God must have a body, or
there could be no body to anything. Doubtless He
has both a "spiritual body" and a "natural body,"
after which ours are patterned.

Christ, the eternal Word, in whom the Divine essence takes form, as our thoughts and emotions take
form in language, is the heavenly, or "celestial body"
of God. Then succeeds the more solid (though in reality more insubstantial) form of what we call Nature;
and yet we know nothing more of what nature really
is than we do what our souls are made of. We only
know that there is Life, and a Manifestation of
life in multitudinous and necessarily related forms.

Many of these forms in which Life shows itself to itself appear to be convertible; and for aught we know to the contrary our entire physical being, or the shadowing forth of our essential soul-life, may be converted back into the original gaseous, or semi-spiritual, or even the purely spiritual substance from which we suppose all things to have arisen. There may be literal truth in the strange expression, "The Word was made flesh and dwelt among us."

There is an unwrought mine of significance in this favorite epithet of the most spiritual minded of all the apostles   Consider what that primary factor of our intellectual life is which we call a *word*, and through what marvelous changes we can cause it to pass in a few moments.   We first conceive a *form of thought*; that is the Word in its pure spiritual form. Next we can pronounce it with increasing degrees of emphasis in our minds without any apparent physical action, though there is an action of the brain, deep within.   Then we can whisper it more and more loudly. Then we can resound it, with rising power and varying inflection.   So far the eye beholds nothing, yet a reality is brought forth capable of creating and setting in motion armies of men.   But the end is not yet. In another moment we can incarnate our Word in a still more materialized form by writing, and send it away from us to the other side of the world.   It is still our Word, our offspring, our begotten child, and carries our spirit wherever it goes, and plants that

spirit, and begets a spiritualized image of itself, in
other minds, one, two or a thousand. And after all
what is it? We call it our book, our letter, our
speech, our Word. It does its errand and may return to us again, and again go forth. You can burn
the book without destroying the Utterance. This
lives on, a spiritual, but a real and potential existence. It has both a natural, or corporeal, body, and
also a spiritual body. What the written letter is to
the thought or sentiment which it shadows forth, that
our flesh and blood encasement seems to be to our
essential soul-life. It helps to accentuate, confirm
and reproduce thought and knowledge. But the
particular form or material of the image that serves
as a reflector of our mental force is a matter of indif-
ference. The original manuscript of the Bible was
long since destroyed. Did that destroy the Bible?
The flesh and blood with which we began life has
several times been replaced to the last particle. But
we still have a body, and in a sense the same body;
because when reduced to the last analysis the body
is not matter, but a certain *form of being*; just as a
word is a *form of thought.*

Now Christ had such a body before he appeared to
to the eyes of men in Judea. God clothed that body
with a covering of flesh, and still further with an emblematic dress, in which he taught mankind certain
vitally important lessons. But when the dress and
the flesh were removed the body of Christ was not

destroyed. He still exists and does all things as the Son and Word of God, and has long since returned and entered into the life of the world, and has made another body for himself in his Church, as he is himself the Word or spiritual Embodiment of God. And he even continues to incarnate himself anew in successive generations of his disciples; just as the Bible, which is a verbal incarnation of the truth, passes through edition after edition, with new ink and paper, but is the same glorious Book of Divine Revelation through all, its form, or *body of sacred learning*, being a spiritual subsistance.

Christ's coming is therefore a *continuous process of drawing nearer and nearer to the understanding and heart of mankind.* And when the clouds of human ignorance and superstition shall have all passed away, then we shall " know him even as we are known of him;" then shall we be "like him for we shall see him as he is." And when we "awake in his likeness" we shall be satisfied."

XXI.

THE SEPARATION.

A dark pall, resembling the shadow of death, fell
on the Society of Friends in America in 1827-28.
The event is thus spoken of by the historian of the
Society Samuel M. Janney, who has labored to make
an accurate record of the circumstances, though his
account naturally favors the division to which he was
attached. It is to be found in the Fourth Volume of
his History of Friends, divided from the main work,
as though it were an episode which happily might
some day be forgotten and erased from the records of
a people whose name it has been thought to dishonor.

The separation that took place in the Society of
Friends in America, during the years 1827 and '28,
was an event of deep and painful interest to its members, and is still regarded by many, both within and
without its pale, as a subject of unceasing regret. It
was accompanied by alienation of feeling among many
who had long been knit together in the closest ties of
friendship, and it diminished the salutary influence
that the Society had always exerted from the first
settlement of the country in the promotion of every
work that tended to the public good.

"The separation was preceded by an exciting controversy, in which the doctrines and discipline of the Society were discussed, both parties claiming to hold the tenets and to act upon the principles of the early Friends."

The historian then enters into an elaborate examination of those doctrines of the Society which were brought into controversy, seeking to gather these, since there never had been a formal creed adopted, from the writings of leading members, among whom, it is admitted that there were, from the first, "some shades of difference,—they did not all see 'eye to eye,' neither was such uniformity of sentiment considered essential to religious union; for being united in Christ, through the bond of the Spirit, all minor differences were deemed unimportant, or regarded only as incentives to Christian charity."

What a blessing to the Society and to mankind had the sentiment just quoted been more generally acted upon, not only in relation to matters of doctrine, but to those minor testimonies, in maintenance of which even the charitable Friends were not slow to cut off and exclude those who differed from the unwritten creed of the main body! So hard is it to see the beam in our own eye while plucking at the mote in a brother's eye. As compared with the great doctrines of the personality and divinity of Christ and authenticity of the Scriptures which contained the explosive material that burst the Society in twain,

setting "the father against the son and the son against
the father, the mother against the daughter, and the
daughter against the mother," how trivial were those
questions of language and dress, of music, and methods in marriage, which had so often been made the occasion of infringing just liberty and separating brethren.   And when those underlying causes which are
the true seeds of mysterious events come up for judgment, it may be discovered that a practice so inconsistent with their lofty profession had not escaped the
impartial eye of Him who is no respecter of persons
or societies, but who will "reward every one according as his work shall be."

As the dissolution of the American Union was
God's judgment against oppression, so the dissolution of nearly every religious society in this land of
boasted liberty of conscience may fairly be considered
as God's visitation upon His oppressive Church.
This general judgment against both the church and
state was the subject of what seems a well authenti-
cated prophecy given in the form of a vision to a
member of the Society of Friends named Joseph
Hoag, in 1803. In describing his vision he says,
" And when the dividing spirit entered the Society of
Friends it raged in as high degree as in any I had
noticed or before discovered." As the Friends had
sinned against the bright light of their own lofty professions, this was but just; and the great catas-
trophe is therefore less to be regretted than the

causes which led to it: and even these afford but another
illustration of the general tendencies of human society.

It is not my purpose to give a history, or even a
sketch of the notable event under consideration, beyond stating generally that the Society in this country
divided into two sections, by the withdrawal, sometimes of one and sometimes of the other party. Those
who disapproved of the movement against Elias Hicks
and his friends were in several Yearly Meetings the
larger portion of the Society, and chose to be called
simply Friends, but were generally termed Hicksites
by their opponents who assumed the title of Orthodox Friends. Great confusion and distress resulted
from the separation, and occasionally the civil courts
were appealed to; but in most instances an amicable
adjustment of claims was effected so that the two
companies either worshipped separately, for a time,
in the same house, or, with an equitable division of
property, built another house near by: and thereafter
each party pursued its course in almost total oblivion
of the affairs of the other. It can scarcely be said
that love and charity abounded, or have yet risen to
the point of "esteeming other better than themselves." There is, however, a very decided ameliora-
tion in feeling, approximating in some cases to an
inward reunion; and were it possible to bring their
views more into harmony a reconciliation could perhaps be effected. But the very act of separation
drove them more and more aloof from each other on

the points held in controversy, insomuch that it was remarked that "One party is on the gallop for Rome, while the other has taken the long trot toward Constantinople."

Elias Hicks, to whose radical views more than to any other single cause the separation was probably due, is said to have remarked that he "feared his friends more than his enemies." He is also credited with the illustration, in apology for some statements of his own which he recognized to have an extreme tendency, that "if one would straiten a crooked stick he bends it backward more than strait." It was the persuasiveness and power of Elias Hick's eloquence combined with a not thoroughly digested theology, and a free, bold manner of throwing out fragmentary conceptions, after the method of speculative geniuses in general, which fanned the smouldering elements of discord into an open flame, or at least made the occasion of their outburst. A reverse movement of theologic tendencies in England had carried the Society of Friends there into closer affiliation with the Anglican Church on some points of doctrine than was originally the case. This drift of the English body toward what are commonly regarded as orthodox views had culminated and found expression in the writings of Joseph John Gurney whose talents, character and philanthropic works had won universal respect, and several of whose brothers and sisters had joined the Episcopal Church, giving him no doubt a strong inclination to cultivate unity of sentiments and views with that body, so far as possible. A slight shudder of opposition had been manifested in both England and Ireland, causing a limited separation in the latter country; but the general trend toward orthodoxy was overpowering and secured virtual unity in the Society throughout Great Britain. In America the case was different. The body here had been nurtured largely on the writings of the early Friends, and the genius of liberty had perhaps increased the range of free thought until it verged, in some instances, on license. Aware of this condition, missionaries from the Society in England came to rescue their brethren in America, and, if the history be correct, were so energetic in their office as to precipitate the dissensions into open discord. Had they possessed a gift for reconciliation, and understood the disease they strove to cure, the result might have been very different. For though extreme views no doubt did exist and were to some extent openly promulgated, the trouble could not be removed by force, or by the enchantments of church discipline; and it was this vain endeavor which placed the "orthodox" party in the wrong in some instances. Many among Friends who did not sympathize with the particular opinions which caused the controversy felt that the rights of private judgment were being assailed, and that charity was more essential to the Church than uniformity of doctrine.

There can be no doubt, on the other hand, that serious, and not altogether causeless, alarm was felt for the integrity of doctrines deemed essential to the religious life of the Society, and to its wholesome influence. Both parties were sincere; and the earnestness of their convictions made the struggle more intense, and reconciliation almost hopeless from the first.

The decree had gone forth, and the woful line of separation was drawn through the Society, often cutting it into very unequal divisions. New England, and the South, below the national Capital, remained united to the Orthodox branch, while in New York and Pennsylvania the preponderance was largely with the other division.

The event has been very generally regretted in its causes and consequences, and has been thought by impartial observers to have weakened both divisions, not only in numbers and influence, but also in purity of faith and doctrine. The venerable poet Whittier has recently given expression to this statement in the following letter, in reply to an invitation to be present at a centennial celebration where members of both societies were to take a part.

Holderness, N. H., 7*th mo.* 20, 1885.
R. S. HAVILAND;
Dear Friend:—It is not possible for me to be present at the Centennial celebration of the Chap-

paqua Monthly Meeting. It will be an occasion of
much interest, and I would be glad to be with you.
I am pleased to see that both branches of the old Society will participate in it, and I infer from this that
the old bitter feeling between them has greatly
changed. The separation should never have taken
place, and the results of it have been evil. Both divisions have in consequence somewhat strayed from
the old paths trodden by Fox and Penn and Barclay.
Let us hope that the time is coming when both will
retrace their steps and stand together on the vital
principle of Quakerism, avoiding Calvinism on the
one hand and "free religion" on the other.

With thanks for the invitation, I am very truly thy
friend

JOHN G. WHITTIER.

Whether the hope so fittingly expressed is ever to
be realized, seems at present not a little doubtful.
The feeling of the parties has indeed very considera-
bly improved, but the mental discords are nearly as
great as ever. To each of them the other seems more
widely astray even than the denominations against
which they formerly contended together. One charges the other with infidelity in discrediting portions of
the Bible, in denying the atonement, or its compen-
satory sacrifice, and in robbing Jesus of his divinity; while the other thinks the first has grown
more outward and literal in some respects than

even the Calvinists, while in practice it has lost many of the distinctive features of Quakerism, and scarcely deserves the title. So that although the words selected by the honored poet to characterize their divergent tendencies may sound a little harsh to both parties they are justified by the estimate in which each holds the other. The words, "Calvinism" and "free religion," were no doubt used in a somewhat "free" sense, one for a strict adherence to literal renderings of the Bible, and the other for a cutting loose from the essence as well as the letter of Scripture doctrine. And I trust the previous pages will assist the discerning reader to see that there is ample justification for the judgment thus kindly passed. Not by any means that all in either division have thus deviated. This would be far from the truth and must not be inferred. But the *tendency* toward opposite extremes has been unmistakable; and it only affords another illustration of a well known law of mind and matter.

To those who have read thoughtfully the preceding pages it may occur that nearly all the errors of the Society of Friends can be classed under the general head of Extremes. *Extremism* may be said to have well nigh ruined a once happy and flourishing society. Should the time ever come when they can consent to return to the "golden mean" of simple, practical, spiritual truth, the "Healer of Breaches" may again cause His face to shine upon them and

bless them.   In that case they will once more become
what their principles seem well calculated to make
them, a leading power for good in the world.

XXII.

SUMMARY.

What then are the essential features of the religious system known as Quakerism? They are—

1. The Manifestation of the Life and Light of Christ to the soul and mind of man, for his redemption from sin and its effects, and his guidance in the path of duty, the world over:—This is the "corner stone, elect, precious."

2. The Scriptures contain a true history of the dealings of God with some who have received this Light, and most important revelations of the Divine mind and purposes with respect to individuals, nations, and mankind at large. They are thus the Words of God, but are effective for good only as they are interpreted and applied by that Word of God who is the soul of life and knowledge.

3. Inasmuch as "God was in Christ, reconciling the world unto Himself;" and Jesus said, "He that hath seen me hath seen the Father;" and again, "Believe me that I am in the Father, and the Father in me;" and again, "I will pray the Father and He shall give you another Comforter, that He may abide with you forever, even the Spirit of Truth;" and

again, " I will not leave you comfortless, I will come
to you:" therefore, the Father, Son and Spirit are
united in one heavenly BEING, one eternal, all-
pervading Substance, Form and Life ; which Being is
One and yet Diverse, like all its issues, and is, in all
its members and its issues, characterized by personal,
or self, knowledge as an indispensable attribute of
spiritual existence, so that whoever is of God says *I*
and *Thou* and *We*.

4. All true worship and divine service must be
performed under the impulse, and by direction of the
Spirit of God, with the use of such means as He may
recommend to the enlightened understanding.

5. The Spirit thus appoints to every one his appropriate work and office, qualifies each for his duty,
and inspires the willing heart to its performance.
When such quickening is not felt the soul should rev-
erently " watch unto prayer," and wait, as a servant
for the orders of his master. But general duties, for
which a permanent qualification has been obtained,
may be discharged in the light of established principles and sanctified reason.

6. As "the head of every man is Christ," or in the
words of Jesus, "One is your Master, even Christ,
and all ye are brethren," all members of the Christian household stand on an essential equality, and
should do their work freely unto the Lord, as grace
is freely given—not contracting with man as though
they were servants of men, or entitled to re-

wards. Nevertheless, the same law of brotherly
equality in love and duty requires that each shall
share in the needful labors and expenses of the common service, according to the talents God has placed
in his trust. And this should be done in a way to
insure the highest efficiency and well-being of the
whole body.

7. Woman is called to be a helpmate for man in
the Church as well as the Home: and though sin
and a low state of society have long placed her at a
disadvantage, it is the office of Christianity to restore
her to her rightful position, and insure her the free
use of all the faculties of her being for her own and
the common benefit.

8. As Jesus Christ is the Prince of Peace, the
Lamb of God, who alone can take away the sin of the
world, and as He laid down His life rather than resist His enemies with force, it is inconsistent with
the spirit of His religion for His disciples to engage
in war. Nor should they resist any kind of wrong
with violence, or legal weapons, when, by the use of
moral agencies, evil can be overcome with good, and
a higher blessing secured.

9. Plainness, candor, and simplicity are among
the brightest ornaments of the Christian character,
and should be exemplified in language, manners, apparel, and temperate modes of living.

10. Good works, though they do not, except as an
undeveloped element of faith, or as faith itself, form

the beginnings of spiritual life, are yet an indispensable result of the presence of divine grace in the heart. Hence though pardon is not obtained thereby, being the fruit of God's paternal love and mercy, yet is no man justified, in a proper sense of the word, until he becomes just and brings forth "works meet for repentance," neither sin nor righteousness being imputed by God where they do not really exist. "This is the work of God that ye believe on Him, whom He hath sent."

11. The saving virtue of the Atonement consists, not in the vicarious suffering which His assumption of humanity brought on Christ through the necessary ties of associated being, but in the meritorious faith and obedience which fulfilled the laws man had broken, and the self-sacrificing love wherein He gave Himself to be the life of the world, becoming, in His heavenly nature, both a fountain of new impulses, and food for all man's regenerated affections and powers. Being thus renewed in the image of God by an actual birth of Christ in the soul, man is reconciled to God, and at length fully reunited with him as an acceptable member of Christ's body, "through the blood of the everlasting covenant."

12. Man, thus reinstated in life, under a perfect and competent Head, should go on to perfection, persevering unto the end, which is eternal life. And so fast as he outgrows the various helps and means of instruction which God, as a wise Father, appoints for

his use, these should be exchanged for instruments adapted to his condition and understanding. This is the organic law of Christ's Kingdom, which kingdom is already in the world progressively. Under the operation of this law typical rites will naturally give place to the more convenient symbolism of language, and the object lessons of daily life, in which historic and abstract truths may readily be embodied as food and stimulus to the understanding and the heart. No other authority is needed for the discontinuance of any outward rite than proof of its present inutility ; and vice versa. "In essentials unity, in non-essentials liberty, in all things charity."

The above propositions, though expressed in different language from that commonly used, seem to me to embody the substance of what is distinctively called Quaker doctrine. On the subjects of the Divine nature and the Atonement I have formulated the statements with a view to the fuller development of ideas imperfectly unfolded, but which may be found in the system, if carefully examined. I would ask the candid reader if they do not present a most reasonable compendium of Vital Christianity, divested of what is necessarily transitory in a religion designed for such a race of beings as men?—The creature of a day, born in poverty, nurtured in ignorance and vice, rising slowly, amid conflicting influences, without and within, to a contemplation of his nature, condition,

relations and prospects, but evermore accumulating
for himself and his posterity the data of more exact
and comprehensive knowledge, the individual man
seems to merge his life, without losing his identity,
in the on-rolling tide of race-existence which, with all
its defilements and noise and foam, age by age, as its
channel widens and deepens, grows somewhat purer,
and reflects more fairly the face of the expanding
heaven—such is the being God has taken to train for
eternity, until he shall reflect not only the beauty of
Nature but the varied grace and glory of the eternal
Sun of Righteousness. What changes must needs
come to him in the long process of thought's unfold-
ing from the tiny green bud of his boyhood visions to
the full-blown flower of manly wisdom. What going
forward and backward, what turnings round and
round, what putting on and taking off, what clinging
to the old and accepting the new, what overturnings,
conflicts, storm and death might we not expect ere
Peace, with dove-like wing, coming from Heaven,
shall rest with abiding light on the sons of God and
man. Such has ever been, and such will yet a long
time be, the experience of mankind, even in its most
favored portions.

Let us now endeavor to summarize what has been
offered in friendly criticism on the supposed mistakes
of the Society of Friends. It has been observed that
they nearly all fall under one general head which
may be defined as the *Tendency to Extremes.* It may

also be observed that most of these supposed blemishes were a growth commencing very soon after the rise of the Society and continuing indefinitely. But a reaction has in some instances already set in.

1. In seeking to be guided by the Inner Light of the Spirit the Friends failed to make a full use of previous revelations of that Spirit as a corresponding Outward Light, "profitable for doctrine, for reproof, for correction, and for instruction in righteousness." The Bible, though privately read, and freely commended and quoted in public, was crowded from its natural and appropriate place in the public services through fear of its being used formally. And thus the "candle of the Lord," which should ever be kept burning before the altar, not being provided with a candlestick and oil from the reservoirs of divine wisdom, sometimes went out and the people were left in darkness, or fed with a few flickerings from the dry wick of the human understanding and memory.

2. While striving to avoid formalities in worship they fell into a formal quietism unprofitable to the ordinary mind. This arose, not from dependence on the Spirit, but from inattention to its gentler motions. Had they stepped into the pool when "the angel first troubled the waters," or risen when the Master first bade them take up their bed and walk, they would have been healed, and the people would have received instruction.

3. Claiming to preach by inspiration ministers

came to depend on the Spirit to furnish them both inspiration and knowledge. Not being able to get the latter in that way, they were tempted to supply the deficiency by empty conceits or wearisome repetitions. Learning and mental discipline thus becoming neglected, the right arm of the church lost much of its power and efficiency. Meantime the theory that ministers, being furnished gratuitously by the Spirit for their work, should give in like manner, refusing all compensation for time, and all regular aid for the support of themselves and their families, confirmed the evil, and left many parts of the vineyard without "a man to till the ground." True "there went up a mist from the earth and watered the whole face of the ground," but this did not prove sufficient for the more tender plants of Christian culture, which need "rain from heaven" in ample and somewhat uniform supply.

4. Prayer, though existing in substance, often failed to find adequate expression, so that the soul of the congregation rose not as the voice of one man to commune with God and ask things meet for the common need. The fire that comes not to a blaze, though it may keep itself warm, will seldom warm a church sufficiently in this wintry world. There is danger also that it may go out, or remain unfelt, like dormant coals amid the ashes.

5. "Out of the abundance of the heart the mouth speaketh; and where the Christian's heart is full of

love and joy there is no form of expression more natural, and inspiring to like feelings in others, than sacred song. The voice of the ages testifies to the power of song as a gift of Heaven for the world's uplifting; and merely because it is easily perverted from its highest uses Christians should not neglect an instrument so gratifying to the pure heart, and so powerful for good as the melody which echoes back the joys of Heaven.

6. The word "Plainness" has been used to represent and enforce practices which long since should have ceased to be regarded as binding on the conscience, or made a test of social standing. The conversion of the Church of Christ into a society of language and dress reform has hedged the entering path to the Quaker fold with needless thorns, turned thousands of the young into other pastures, and kept tens of thousands from looking toward it as a desirable home for religious association.

7. The uncalled-for severity of the Discipline in other respects, and especially in regard to the marriage relations, intensified the evils of ecclesiastical misrule to such a pitch that liberty, once the darling of the Quaker household, at length fled the gates of this meek-eyed daughter of Zion, and took refuge with her late enemies.

8. The principle of full birthright membership, without the requisites of positive faith and experience, strengthened the existing disorders by placing the af-

fairs of the Church to some extent in the hands of
unconverted persons, and by putting stones instead
of coals on the gospel fire.

9. The spiritualizing tendency at length devel-
oped extremes of doctrine on points of vital interest
to religion, which, with the efforts made to repress
them, finally destroyed the unity of the Body, impair-
ing its credit and usefulness, and impelling the in-
flamed sections still further toward opposite poles of
thought and sentiment.

10. Contrary to the intentions of its founders, the
Society gradually built up walls on every side and
became one of the most exclusive of the Protestant
sects. So rigidly has its exclusive policy been en-
forced, in order to shut out anticipated danger, that
in some cases it has shut in enemies it sought
to exclude, and deprived itself of the benefits it might
have received from others, while at the same time its
influence for good has been limited by unwillingness
to meet brethren of other names in the open field of
friendly intercourse and discussion, under the banner
of Christian love and charity. Truth needs no defence but the sword of the Spirit.

The above appear to me to be the most important
general causes of the Decline in the Society of
Friends. And surely are they not enough? What
body not formed of good materials could have stood
for two centuries against such influences?

In enumerating these causes it is not proper to include the universal sources of spiritual weakness and want. Human nature is the same in all times and places. "Individual unfaithfulness" is not peculiar to one society or age more than another; nor are the general temptations of worldliness, wealth, pleasure-seeking, and the like, different now from what they have always been. We cannot suppose a general decline of faith and church-enterprise without having this also to account for. God is able to stir up His people now as well as at other times. But if He sees that all their limbs are fettered why should He trouble them, till they discover their errors and lay aside their chains? When ancient Israel refused to go forward into the land of Promise and God turned them back into the wilderness they were obliged to remain there until the generation that rebelled was dead. Then their children advanced by way of the Jordan, under Joshua, the successor of Moses, and inherited the promises made to Abraham. This great historic parable is evermore repeated in human experience, and may perhaps be again illustrated in the fortunes of this "peculiar people" who in several respects closely resemble the literal seed of Abraham—called in the Spirit to the adoption of sons, but brought under bondage to the forms of law, esteeming all others aliens, and yet living to see those they despised enter the broad fields of Gospel liberty before themselves. What a lesson of humility and charity should all this teach us.

Nor is it at all probable that a Society which has always disclaimed sectarianism and yet has shut its heart against its sister denominations because of certain differences of opinion will be allowed to build up an exclusive order, contrary to the spirit of Christianity and of the age of freedom. All these things must be repented of, and the great High Priest and Bishop of Souls, who has broken down the walls of partition and rent the veil from before the Ark of Testimony, must be accepted for a Leader, in the way of His coming, before prosperity can again be known in the House of Benjamin.

Featured Titles from Westphalia Press

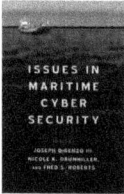

Issues in Maritime Cyber Security Edited by Nicole K. Drumhiller, Fred S. Roberts, Joseph DiRenzo III and Fred S. Roberts

While there is literature about the maritime transportation system, and about cyber security, to date there is very little literature on this converging area. This pioneering book is beneficial to a variety of audiences looking at risk analysis, national security, cyber threats, or maritime policy.

The Rise of the Book Plate: An Exemplative of the Art by W. G. Bowdoin, Introduction by Henry Blackwel

Bookplates were made to denote ownership and hopefully steer the volume back to the rightful shelf if borrowed. They often contained highly stylized writing, drawings, coat of arms, badges or other images of interest to the owner.

The Great Indian Religions by G. T. Bettany

G. T. (George Thomas) Bettany (1850-1891) was born and educated in England, attending Gonville and Caius College in Cambridge University, studying medicine and the natural sciences. This book is his account of Brahmanism, Hinduism, Buddhism, and Zoroastrianism

Unworkable Conservatism: Small Government, Freemarkets, and Impracticality by Max J. Skidmore

Unworkable Conservatism looks at what passes these days for "conservative" principles—small government, low taxes, minimal regulation—and demonstrates that they are not feasible under modern conditions.

A Place in the Lodge: Dr. Rob Morris, Freemasonry and the Order of the Eastern Star by Nancy Stearns Theiss PhD

Ridiculed as "petticoat masonry," critics of the Order of the Eastern Star did not deter Rob Morris' goal to establish a Masonic organization that included women as members. As Rob Morris (1818-1888) came "into the light," he donned his Masonic apron and carried the ideals of Freemasonry through a despairing time of American history.

Demand the Impossible: Essays in History as Activism
Edited by Nathan Wuertenberg and William Horne

Demand the Impossible asks scholars what they can do to help solve present-day crises. The twelve essays in this volume draw inspiration from present-day activists. They examine the role of history in shaping ongoing debates over monuments, racism, clean energy, health care, poverty, and the Democratic Party.

International or Local Ownership?: Security Sector
Development in Post-Independent Kosovo
by Dr. Florian Qehaja

International or Local Ownership? contributes to the debate on the concept of local ownership in post-conflict settings, and discussions on international relations, peacebuilding, security and development studies.

The Bahai Movement: A Series of Nineteen Papers
by Charles Mason Remey

Charles Mason Remey (1874-1974) was the son of Admiral George Collier Remey and grew up in Washington DC. He studied to be an architect at Cornell (1893-1896) and the Ecole des Beaux Arts in Paris (1896-1903), where he learned about the Baha'i faith, and quickly adopted it.

Ongoing Issues in Georgian Policy and Public Administration
Edited by Bonnie Stabile and Nino Ghonghadze

Thriving democracy and representative government depend upon a well functioning civil service, rich civic life and economic success. Georgia has been considered a top performer among countries in South Eastern Europe seeking to establish themselves in the post-Soviet era.

Poverty in America: Urban and Rural Inequality and
Deprivation in the 21st Century
Edited by Max J. Skidmore

Poverty in America too often goes unnoticed, and disregarded. This perhaps results from America's general level of prosperity along with a fairly widespread notion that conditions inevitably are better in the USA than elsewhere. Political rhetoric frequently enforces such an erroneous notion.

westphaliapress.org

www.ingramcontent.com/pod-product-compliance
Lightning Source LLC
Chambersburg PA
CBHW031532040426
42445CB00010B/499